Advanced Soccer Drills

Colin E. Schmidt
Director of Coaching
Table Mountain Soccer Association

Human Kinetics

Library of Congress Cataloging-in-Publication Data

Schmidt, Colin E., 1966-
Advanced soccer drills / Colin E. Schmidt.
p. cm.
ISBN 0-88011-614-5
1. Soccer--Training. I. Title.
GV943.9.T7S35 1997
796.334'07'7--dc21

96-46416
CIP

ISBN: 0-88011-614-5

Photos on pages iv and x courtesy of University of North Carolina Sports Information; photos on pages xiv, 32, and 154 courtesy of University of Portland Sports Information; photos on pages 66, 108, and 149 courtesy of Indiana University/Guy Zimmer; photo on page 146 © Mary Langenfeld.

Developmental Editor: Marni Basic; **Assistant Editors:** John Wentworth and Alesha G. Thompson; **Editorial Assistant:** Amy Carnes; **Copyeditor:** Denelle Eknes; **Proofreader:** Jim Burns; **Graphic Designer:** Robert Reuther; **Graphic Artist:** Angela K. Snyder; **Photo Editor:** Boyd LaFoon; **Cover Designer:** Jack Davis; **Photographer (cover):** Anthony Neste; **Illustrator:** Sara Wolfsmith; **Printer:** United Graphics

Human Kinetics books are available at special discounts for bulk purchase. Special editions or book excerpts can also be created to specification. For details, contact the Special Sales Manager at Human Kinetics.

Printed in the United States of America 10 9 8 7 6 5 4 3 2

Human Kinetics
Web site: http://www.humankinetics.com/

United States: Human Kinetics
P.O. Box 5076
Champaign, IL 61825-5076
1-800-747-4457
e-mail: humank@hkusa.com

Canada: Human Kinetics, Box 24040
Windsor, ON N8Y 4Y9
1-800-465-7301 (in Canada only)
e-mail: humank@hkcanada.com

Europe: Human Kinetics, P.O. Box IW14
Leeds LS16 6TR, United Kingdom
(44) 1132 781708
e-mail: humank@hkeurope.com

Australia: Human Kinetics
57A Price Avenue
Lower Mitcham, South Australia 5062
(08) 277 1555
e-mail: humank@hkaustralia.com

New Zealand: Human Kinetics
P.O. Box 105-231, Auckland 1
(09) 523 3462
e-mail: humank@hknewz.com

This book is dedicated to Jenny . . .
may she realize all that she dreams,
and all that she works hard to achieve.

Courtesy of University of North Carolina Sports Information

Contents

Drill Finder

Drill #	Drill	Combination Passing	Crosses	Defensive Responsibilities	Dribbling	Goal Scoring & Goalkeeping	Heading	Movement off the Ball	Maintaining Possession	Playing Passes to Feet	Tackling	Winning the Air
1	Cutting and Turning the Ball				✓					✓		
2	Stop and Go				✓							
3	Space Behind the Defender				✓							
4	Fifty-Fifty Ball				✓						✓	
5	Race to the Ball				✓	✓					✓	
6	Facing a Defender				✓	✓					✓	
7	Dribbling With Space Ahead of the Defender				✓						✓	
8	Dribbling on the Wing		✓		✓	✓	✓				✓	
9	Turn and Face				✓					✓	✓	
10	Defender's Dilemma			✓	✓						✓	
11	Shielding				✓				✓		✓	
12	Dribbling to Shoot				✓	✓						
13	Dribbling Against the Goalkeeper				✓	✓						
14	1 vs. 1 Challenge				✓						✓	
15	Dribbling Inside the Defender				✓						✓	
16	Find the Space	✓						✓	✓			
17	Pinball Warm-Up									✓		
18	4 vs. 1 One-Touch Passing								✓	✓		
19	Two-Player Passing Combinations	✓						✓				
20	Dribbling Inside Versus Outside		✓	✓	✓	✓		✓				
21	Double Teamed				✓			✓			✓	
22	Sequential Passing (5 vs. 1)	✓						✓	✓	✓		
23	Across the Grid								✓	✓		
24	Possession or Punishment								✓			
25	Link Pass	✓				✓				✓		
26	Second Pass							✓		✓		
27	Throw-Ins								✓			
28	3 vs. 1 Squared	✓							✓			
29	Restricted Touch Scrimmage	✓						✓				
30	3 vs. 2 (With Point Players)	✓				✓						
31	Tight Marking	✓		✓	✓	✓				✓	✓	
32	Ball Control on the Run					✓						✓
33	Counterclockwise I (Half Field)				✓	✓						
34	Counterclockwise II (Full Field)				✓	✓						

Drill #	Drill	Combination Passing	Crosses	Defensive Responsibilities	Dribbling	Goal Scoring & Goalkeeping	Heading	Movement off the Ball	Maintaining Possession	Playing Passes to Feet	Tackling	Winning the Air
35	Nondominant Leg									✓		
36	Chip Pass					✓						✓
37	Heel Pass	✓				✓		✓				
38	Flick Pass	✓						✓				
39	Long Drives		✓									✓
40	Power-Shot Progression					✓						
41	Quick Shot					✓						
42	Scissors Kick					✓						✓
43	Crossing and Heading to Goal		✓			✓	✓					✓
44	Bending a Pass or Shot					✓						
45	Shooting on the Turn					✓						
46	Side Volleys					✓						✓
47	Controlling Balls Above Knee Height											✓
48	Offensive Heading		✓			✓	✓					✓
49	Defensive Heading						✓					✓
50	Heading Punts						✓					✓
51	Diving Headers						✓					
52	11 vs. 4							✓	✓			
53	Possession Game (5 vs. 5 Plus 2)	✓						✓	✓			
54	Last Goal Wins					✓		✓	✓			
55	Keep-Away With Target Player	✓								✓		
56	Runs From the Back	✓										
57	Point Player (3 vs. 1, 1 vs. 1)	✓				✓						
58	3 vs. 2, 3 vs. 2	✓										
59	Hold the Line			✓		✓						
60	Boxed In (6 vs. 4, 3 vs. 3)					✓					✓	
61	Defending the Penalty Area			✓		✓					✓	✓
62	Throw-Head-Catch						✓					✓
63	Counterattack					✓						
64	Midfielder With Space	✓				✓		✓				
65	Through Ball, Early Cross	✓	✓			✓		✓				
66	Defending the Pass (3 vs. 5)			✓								
67	Marking Up			✓		✓						
68	Forward First (5 vs. 5 Plus 4)	✓				✓		✓	✓	✓		
69	Thinking Player's Restriction							✓				

Acknowledgments

I'd like to thank the players and coaches from Table Mountain Soccer Club in Golden, Colorado, who willingly became a "laboratory" to experiment with new practice drills and ideas. I hope that their discovering the drills that worked compensated for any pain of participating in the ones that didn't.

All the staff and editors at Human Kinetics who worked on the book also have my gratitude. Thanks in particular to Ken Mange and Ted Miller who gave me the opportunity to write the book. Thanks also to Marni Basic, who guided the book from manuscript to completion, and to John Wentworth and Alesha Thompson for their contributions during the editorial process.

Finally, thanks to the universities that contributed photos: UCLA, Indiana, North Carolina, and Portland. Photo editor Boyd LaFoon deserves special recognition for his extra effort in coordinating the photo acquisition.

Introduction

Soccer can be played at many levels. When school children play the game at recess, a player kicks the ball down the field and everyone runs after it. As players develop further, they learn to receive and control the ball. They discover different ways of kicking it. Later, players will decide where to kick it and to whom. They will develop reasons for their actions on the field. This controlled, purposeful soccer is the beginning of what I call a higher level of play.

The soccer drills and games in this book systematically reveal the skills necessary for success at a higher level of play. The focus is on developing the abilities of individual soccer players. The goal is to provide coaches with specific drills to improve the way players handle defensive pressure, the way they see the field, and the way they make decisions in game-related situations.

I wrote the book as a soccer player who later became a soccer coach. I am not a graduate from the school of coaches who were at one time famous, professional players. I played successfully on competitive soccer teams from childhood through college. I was an average player, with brief highlights as an all-state high school player and as a member of the Olympic Development Program.

Years later as a coach and veteran of the game, I can identify where my progress as a player stopped. In a way then, this book reflects my shortcomings as a soccer player. It picks up on the page where I left off on the field. The book identifies skills that players must develop if they want to compete in select soccer programs. The drills reinforce the fundamentals yet aim to uncover the subtleties of the game. They highlight little things to coaches that can distinguish the skilled player from the mediocre.

Chapter 1 isolates the skills necessary for success in 1 vs. 1 situations. The drills place players in the different 1 vs. 1 situations they will face during games. The drills will help players learn to assess these situations and direct play to their own benefit. Whether maintaining possession, dribbling forward, or setting up for a shot or pass, skilled players must develop and practice techniques to maintain the advantage against opponents.

Chapter 2 focuses on vision and decision making, two critical ingredients for smart, purposeful soccer. Before a player receives the ball, he

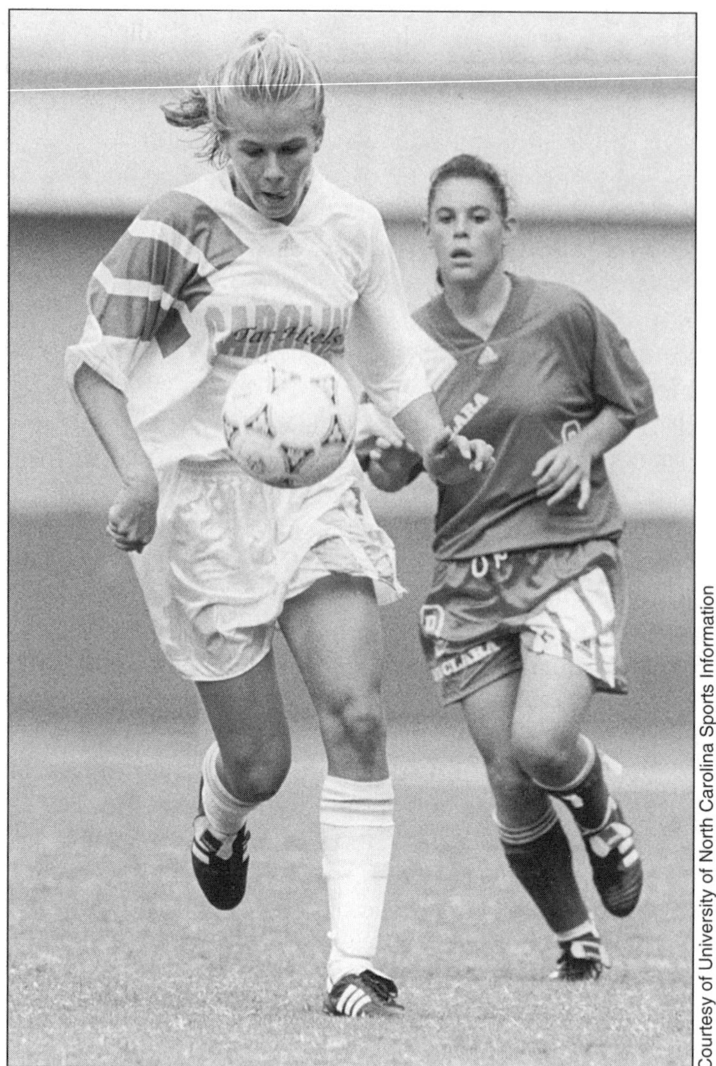

Courtesy of University of North Carolina Sports Information

or she must evaluate the available options. The skilled player must have composure and be able to read the game. The drills in this chapter will help coaches teach players how to see the field and make better decisions under pressure.

Chapter 3 concerns technical soccer skills beyond the fundamentals. The drills here will give players the opportunity to acquire and develop new skills. This chapter will help coaches pinpoint advanced skills and explain situations in which players might use them. Perhaps more important, players may develop a better understanding of their limitations. Skilled players should play to their strengths and avoid or minimize situations that call for skills beyond their abilities.

Chapter 4 brings individual skills into a larger team or tactical framework. The goal here is for players to work together to accomplish a specific task, such as keeping possession of the ball or advancing it toward goal. The drills in this chapter ask that players be cognizant of the purposes of their play in different situations on the field.

Chapter 5 explains different techniques the coach can employ to help players develop the new skills presented in this book. A section on restrictions clarifies why and when a coach can use *conditioned play* to enhance the learning process. The last part of the chapter provides a model for mixing and matching drills to form complete practices.

In chapter 6 an evaluation model is provided for coaches to use when assessing players' abilities 1 vs. 1.

The drills in this book will benefit players who already demonstrate a solid grasp of soccer fundamentals. The age of a player is secondary for many of the drills, but several drills will be more than young players can handle. Players ages 12 and younger should work on the 1 vs. 1 drills in chapter 1, along with a heavy dose of fun games and a steady diet of fundamentals. Younger, more skilled players can also perform some drills in chapter 2. They will not have the physical strength necessary to accomplish some tasks required in chapter 4. Players 12 years old and older can work on most things presented in the book.

One of the jobs of a coach is to identify where a player is in the developmental process. The drills in this book can work as a guide in this process. As you look at each drill and its purpose ask yourself, "Can my players do this?" If not, you've identified a step players can take to reach a higher level of play. The drill finder on pp. vi and vii can help identify the specific skills that each drill highlights.

Developing a skilled player is a complex process. Many factors contribute to a player's success. The book focuses on specific soccer-related skills that a coach can address through training. The coach will also need to consider the *raw material*, or the player's athletic abilities. In the early stages of development, coaches can help players develop balance, coordination, and agility. Some players will have gifted natural abilities; others will need to work hard to improve.

Although skilled players may have moments of brilliance, a player's real value is measured in his or her ability to perform routine tasks consistently with precision and accuracy. Skilled soccer has more to do with composure and smart play than with flashy tricks.

Like anything else in life, it takes time and perseverance to rise to the top. The higher the level of play, the harder it is to make gains. The coach dedicated to helping players reach their potential can use the material presented here to help them improve at every practice.

Key to Diagrams

- - - - - - - -→	Path of run
——⚽——→	Path of pass or shot
⋀⋀⚽⋀⋀→	Path of dribble
O or Z	Offensive player
X	Defensive player
N	Neutral player
T	Target player
S	Server
GK	Goalkeeper

Courtesy of University of Portland Sports Information

CHAPTER 1

Winning 1 vs. 1

One attacker against one defender—the 1 vs. 1—is the foundation of soccer. The game revolves around the player with the ball. The 1 vs. 1 requires ball control both to receive the ball and to advance it against pressure. It requires strength to hold off defenders, speed to burst into open space, and confidence to go for it. The skilled player can handle the defensive challenge and often do something positive with the ball.

The drills in this chapter isolate the 1 vs. 1 into its different manifestations during game situations. A 1 vs. 1 on the wing is different from a 1 vs. 1 in front of the goal. In game situations the player with the ball can be an attacker facing an opponent or a defender trapped near the touchline.

The desired next action, whether a pass, a shot, or continuation of the dribble, distinguishes how a player will face a 1 vs. 1 challenge. The exercises in this chapter require players to recognize these factors and practice the subtle skills required for success in each situation.

Aggressive defensive play is also a part of the 1 vs. 1. Encourage players to use their bodies and go for the ball. As they fight for possession, they learn to transition from offense to defense. These drills will help players gain confidence tackling and winning the ball.

The 1 vs. 1 exercises can improve speed and endurance. As a rule, players need a three-to-one work-to-rest ratio. Intervals of playing time should range from 30 to 90 seconds. Shorter intervals at full intensity with more repetitions increase speed. Durations with prolonged exertion improve endurance. Short lines or one pair of players resting while another pair performs moderates this ratio.

One effective way to organize a practice with an emphasis on 1 vs. 1 skills is to set up several stations. Each station will be a different drill from this chapter. One practice, for example, might have four stations. Players divide into four groups and every 10 or 15 minutes rotate through to a new station. Some of the 1 vs. 1 drills are easier for players to supervise themselves. Other, more complicated drills need the presence of a coach in order to run smoothly.

Lastly, skilled players need dependable dribbling moves or fakes. Players will have an opportunity to become comfortable and proficient with key moves as they perform these drills.

Cutting and Turning the Ball

Purpose

To develop the ability to turn the ball away from a defender

Organization

Square grid 7 to 10 yards on a side; 4 players per grid (3 offense, 1 defense).

Procedure

1. Each player begins in a corner, the three offensive players with balls.
2. Each player takes a turn dribbling at the defender. When one player finishes, the next proceeds. As the defender is approached, the dribbler turns and dribbles back to the corner. The defender is passive. Have players practice cutting the ball back with the inside and outside of both feet.

Key Points

This simple warm-up exercise clearly illustrates an important factor for a player to evaluate when taking on a defender: is there space behind the defender to dribble into? In this case there isn't so the player must turn or cut the ball away.

Often in games, players will dribble past defenders only to realize too late that they are trapped by another defender or by limited space. The player may have gained a few yards, but the team would have been better served if the ball was turned away and played to a supporting player.

Players should practice turning with both feet in both directions. A fake can be performed before the turn as well. The turn should occur just outside tackling range (about two or three yards away from the defender). During the turn, the dribbler positions the body between the ball and the defender. After the turn, the player's head is up to look for options.

Variations

1. Players turn and dribble to another corner.
2. Use one ball per grid. Player turns and passes and play continues. The player follows the pass and plays a passive defender lunging at the ball. The player with the ball dribbles around this player, then confronts the player in the corner.
3. Require players to perform a fake before turning the ball. (A fake kick is the easiest one to perform.)

Cutting and Turning the Ball

O O

O X

7 to 10 yards

7 to 10 yards

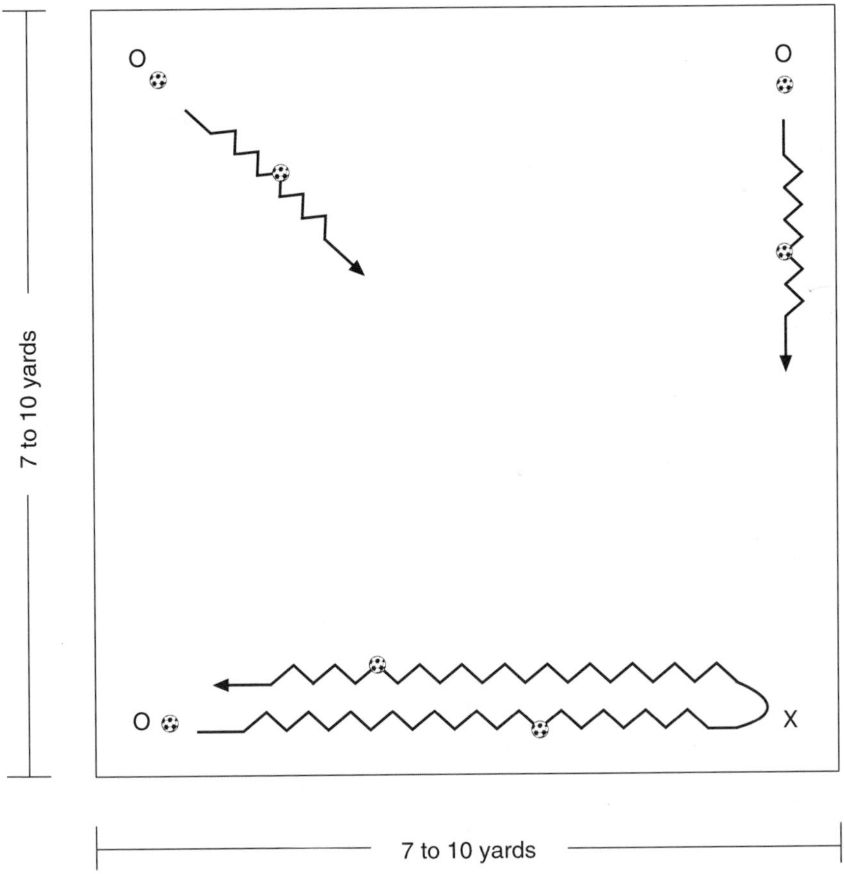

2 Stop and Go

Purpose

To practice changing pace while dribbling

Organization

Players spread out inside a circle 15 to 20 yards in diameter with one ball per player.

Procedure

1. At first players practice dribbling without any restrictions. They practice quick changes of pace, stop-and-go movements, and pushing the ball into pockets of space.
2. At different times have players emphasize a drag of the ball, 90-degree turns, and 180-degree turns. Have them stop the ball, quickly perform one or two unbalancing movements, then proceed with a burst of speed.

Key Points

The stop and go is a wonderful way to commit a defender and create dribbling options. A defender is committed when coming at the ball or when unbalanced. An *unbalancing move* is any body movement or dribbling fake that may succeed in momentarily throwing the defender off balance. A player performs a ball drag by pulling the ball back or to the side with the sole of the foot. Other dribbling moves include fake kicks, step overs, cutting the ball across the body, or dropping the shoulder.

Variations

1. Make players look around and think while dribbling. Ask them questions, such as, "How many players have white socks?" Or give commands like, "Any time I say a word that starts with 'B,' stop the ball, perform a move, and continue." Be creative.
2. Announce acts for players to perform. Give each act a number. Number 1, for example, might be drag the ball backward 180 degrees. Number 2 might be toe touches. Number 3 might be freeze with the right foot on top of the ball, and so on. Call out numbers periodically. Speed up the commands as players get the hang of the drill.
3. On command have players dribble around a distant object and return to the circle.
4. Have players try to kick each other's balls out of the circle. The last one remaining is the winner.
5. Have one or more defenders try to steal the players' balls.

Stop and Go

15 to 20 yards

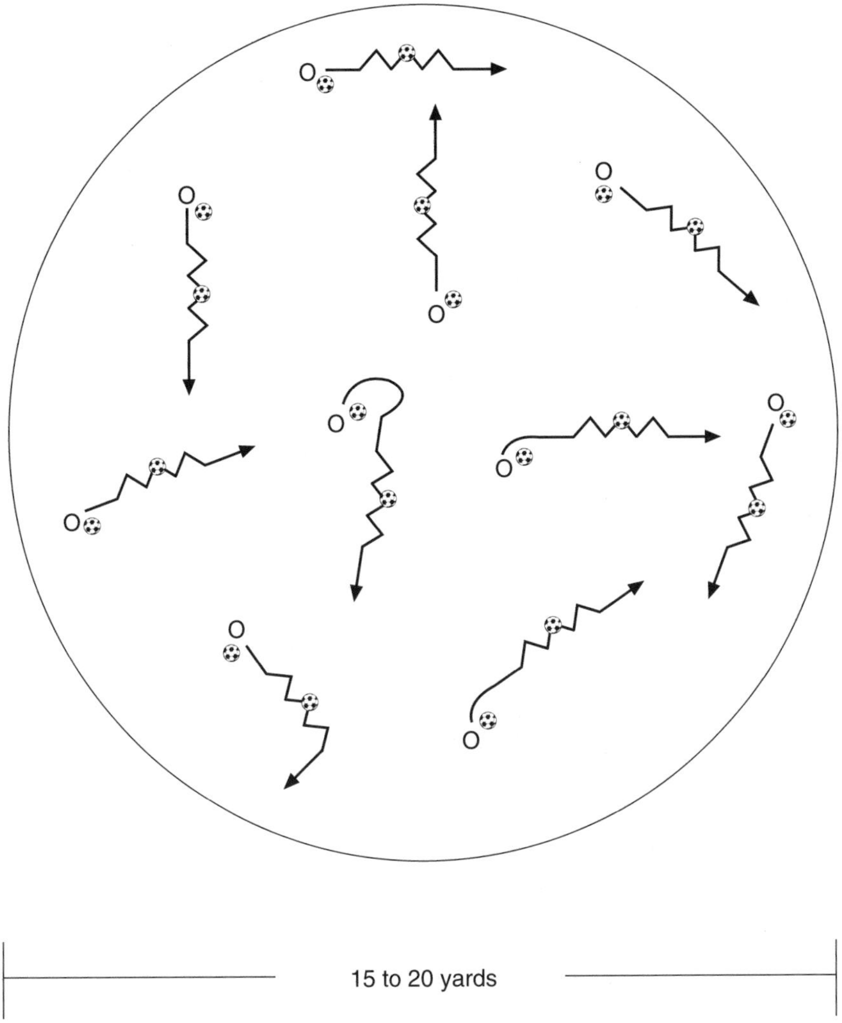

3 Space Behind the Defender

Purpose

To practice dribbling around a defender into space

Organization

Line with 3 players, 10 yards between each player; a player in the middle without a ball.

Procedure

1. A player with a ball starts by passing to the player in the middle.
2. The middle player then tries to dribble past the player who passed the ball.
3. The first player follows the pass into the grid and plays a passive defender. (The defender should lunge at the ball.) The defender is now the middle player.
4. Play continues with a pass from the player on the other side of the grid.

Key Points

The player receiving the pass practices controlling the ball and advancing past a defender. The defender creates pressure by following the pass and lunging at the ball. The lunge is not an attempt to win the ball. The defender performs it for the benefit of the dribbler, who practices pushing the ball past the defender as the defender moves in.

Players should work on the timing of the move. They should accelerate into the space behind the defender. Skilled players are often coached to attack the front foot of the defender. If the defender comes in with the left foot, the dribbler should go to the outside of the defender's left foot. Doing this forces the defender to turn completely around to have another chance at the ball. The dribbler gains time and creates an advantageous situation.

Variations

1. Require players to perform a dribbling fake or move before pushing the ball past the defender.
2. Have the first pass be a throw-in. Increase the distance between players if necessary.

Space Behind the Defender

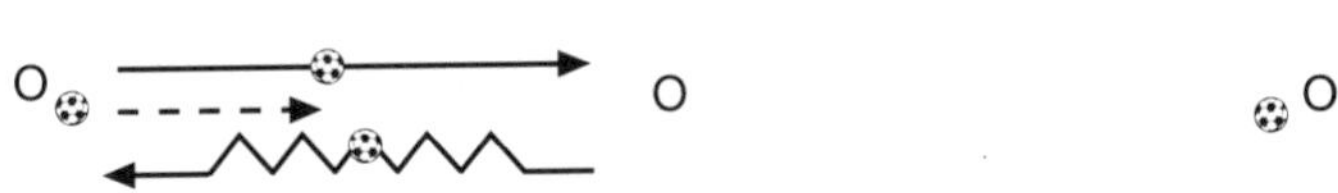

4 Fifty-Fifty Ball

Purpose

To practice winning the ball using a block-tackle and riding the tackle

Organization

Grid 10 by 10 yards, 6 to 8 players per grid. Players form 2 lines, facing one another at opposite sides of the grid. Place 1 ball at the center of the grid.

Procedure

1. On command the two players at the front of each line race to the ball and try to win possession.
2. A point is scored if a player dribbles across the opposite end line.
3. If the ball is kicked out of the grid, neither player receives points.

Key Points

The fifty-fifty ball by definition is one that each player has a chance of winning. Intensity and mental attitude will determine the outcome as much as technique. Both players will likely contact the ball at some time during the turn. The player with the first touch doesn't necessarily have an advantage.

Players should create a firm surface to contact the ball. The center of balance should be low and the body's weight should be balanced over the plant foot so the other foot can make prolonged contact with the ball. The plant foot should be as close to the ball as possible (for a standing, block tackle). The player is trying to *ride the tackle* as the opponent applies pressure. Players will reduce the likelihood of injury if they go in strong and make solid contact with the ball.

Variations

1. Roll the ball into the grid.
2. Serve a bouncing ball into the grid.
3. Change the target area for the dribble. Have players dribble back to their end line or to either side of the grid.

Fifty-Fifty Ball

O
O
O

10 yards

X
X
X

10 yards

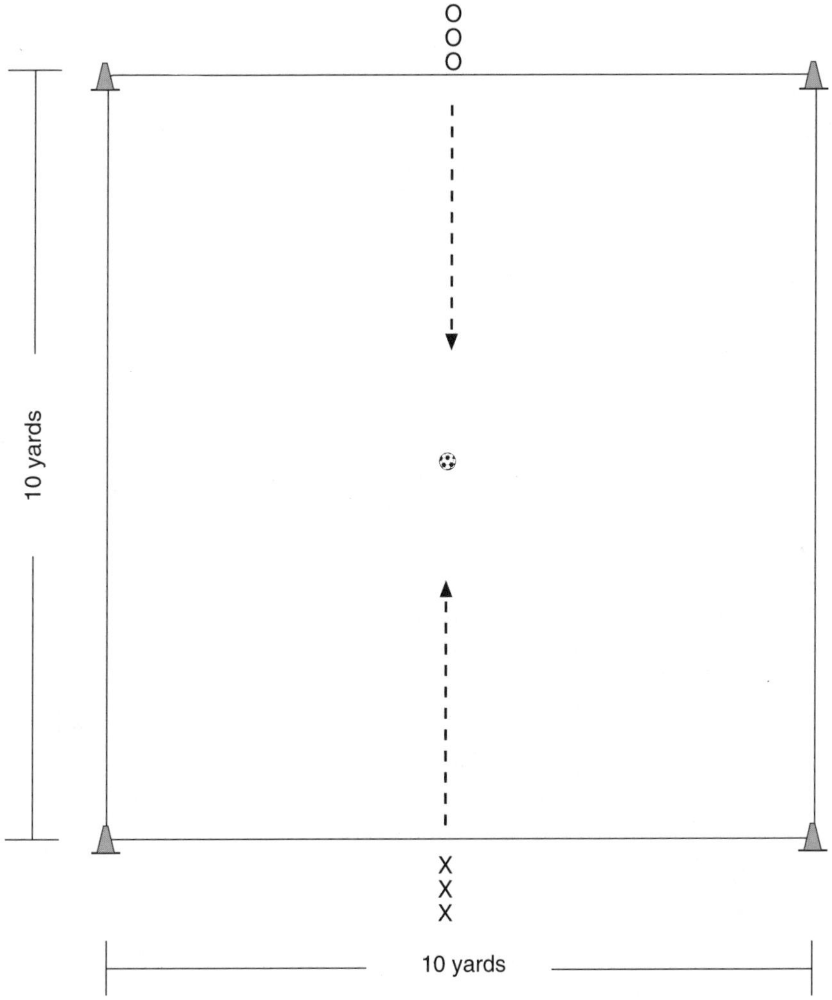

5 Race to the Ball

Purpose

To practice winning shoulder charges, dribbling, and shooting

Organization

Players line up outside of each goalpost. Position a server behind the goal with a supply of balls and a goalkeeper in the goal.

Procedure

1. The server plays a ball into the field 15 to 20 yards from the end line.
2. Each line is a team. At the moment the ball is served, the two players at the front of each line race to the ball as shown in *a* . Both players try to win the ball and score on the same goal. (The player who gets to the ball first tries to beat the other player and score. If the other player wins possession of the ball, he or she then tries to score.)
3. Keep score.

Key Points

Watch closely how the player who reaches the ball first tries to turn and face the defender. A skilled player will turn and face the goal as soon as possible after getting to the ball. Instruct defenders to make it hard for the dribbler to turn and face the goal.

When running at the ball, players can use their upper bodies and shoulders to gain (and keep) possession of the ball. The shoulder tackle is legal only if the player is going straight for the ball. The arm cannot be extended.

To turn with a defender challenging from behind, a player can fake one direction with a shoulder drop or step over, then drag the ball away from the defender with the sole of the foot. While the player is dragging the ball, the body spins to face the goal.

Variations

1. Play without goalkeepers.
2. Pair players of even abilities at the front of each line.
3. Change the starting position of the players or server, as shown in *b*. (For example, players can start near the midfield line.)

Race to the Ball

a

O O O S X X X

GK

b

X X X S O O O

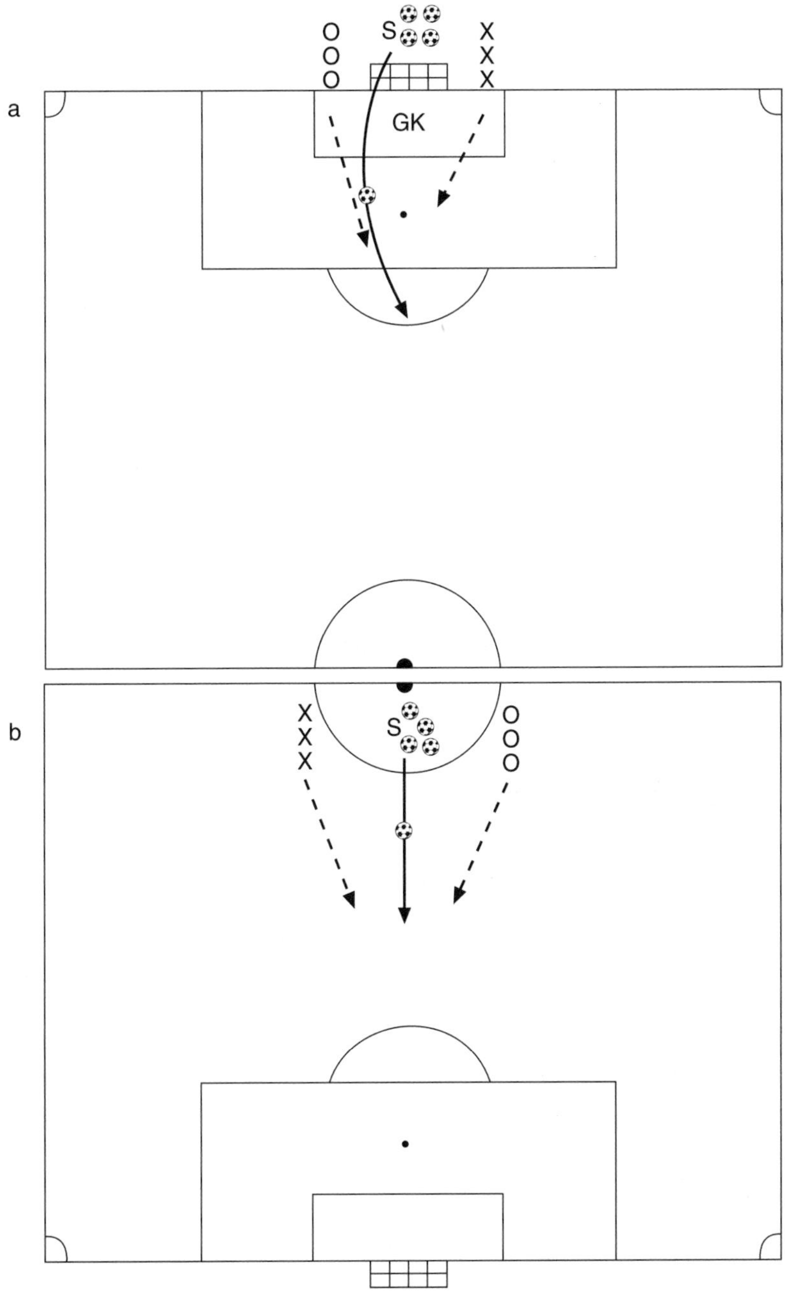

6 Facing a Defender

Purpose

To gain confidence beating an opponent on the run

Organization

Make 2 grids, 1/2 the field in length, 10 to 15 yards in width (from the penalty area to the sidelines); 6 players per grid form 2 lines on opposite ends of each grid.

Procedure

1. The defenders start play by passing and chipping the ball to the player at the front of the attacking line. The player receiving the ball tries to dribble past the defender and across the end line in control of the ball. (Play takes place simultaneously in each grid.)
2. After passing the ball, the defender closes space and tries to gain possession of the ball.
3. If the defender wins the ball, he or she tries to pass it to the player at the end of the grid (the next person in line).

Key Points

Set up long grids in this exercise. Allow players space to run with the ball. The first few touches are important. The level of ball control here will set the tone for what is to come.

As the defender nears, observe what the dribbler does. What parts of the feet are being used? Does the player proceed at the defender? Is there a sharp change of pace or an attempt to fool the defender? The defender succeeds in part if the dribbler delays, stops moving forward, or is forced to the side of the grid.

Variations

1. Player must dribble between either of two small goals set up on the corners of the end lines.
2. Award two points to the dribbler if he or she crosses the end line goalside of the defender (between the defender and the goal) and one point if he or she crosses the end line outside the defender.

Facing a Defender

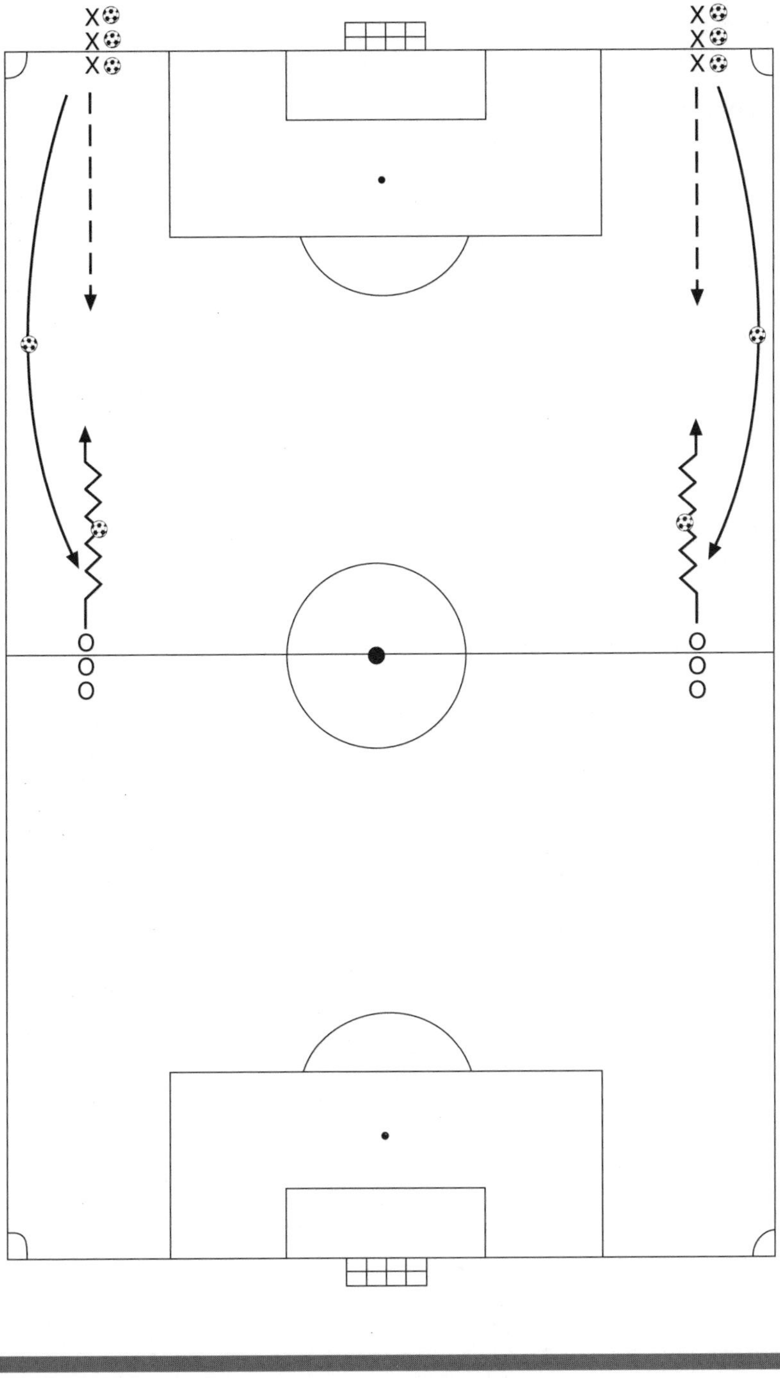

Dribbling With Space Ahead of the Defender

Purpose

To practice dribbling at full speed, maintaining a spatial advantage

Organization

Form 2 lines with 8 to 16 players; 1 line at midfield, the other 7 yards behind and to the outside. Players in the outside line have a supply of balls. Duplicate setup on the other side if more than 5 players per line.

Procedure

1. The first player in the line farthest from goal is the defender. Play starts when this player passes the ball into the space in front of the attacker.
2. The attacker gathers the ball and dribbles toward the goal.
3. The defender tries to tackle the ball or get goalside of the ball.

Key Points

Both players sprint at full speed in this drill. The attacker tries to maintain an advantage with control of the ball; the defender tries to get goalside.

The attacking player should be aware of the defender's position. Attackers should get in the habit of glancing back on occasion. To maintain speed on the dribble, the dribbler should touch the ball with the tops of the feet, toes pointed down. (The feet remain in the same position as when sprinting without a ball.) The ball is touched at the end of the stride.

The defender tries to get goalside and win the ball or force the player away from goal. To perform a slide tackle the defender must come at the ball from the side. The foot and leg create a barrier in front of the ball to stop its momentum. The top leg usually makes contact. The defender can kick the ball out-of-bounds, or better, ride the tackle and keep possession of the ball.

Variations

1. Alter the starting distance of the defender.
2. Attacker gathers the initial pass from a server from another direction.
3. Have the defensive line start inside the attacking line (closer to the center of the field).

Dribbling With Space Ahead of the Defender

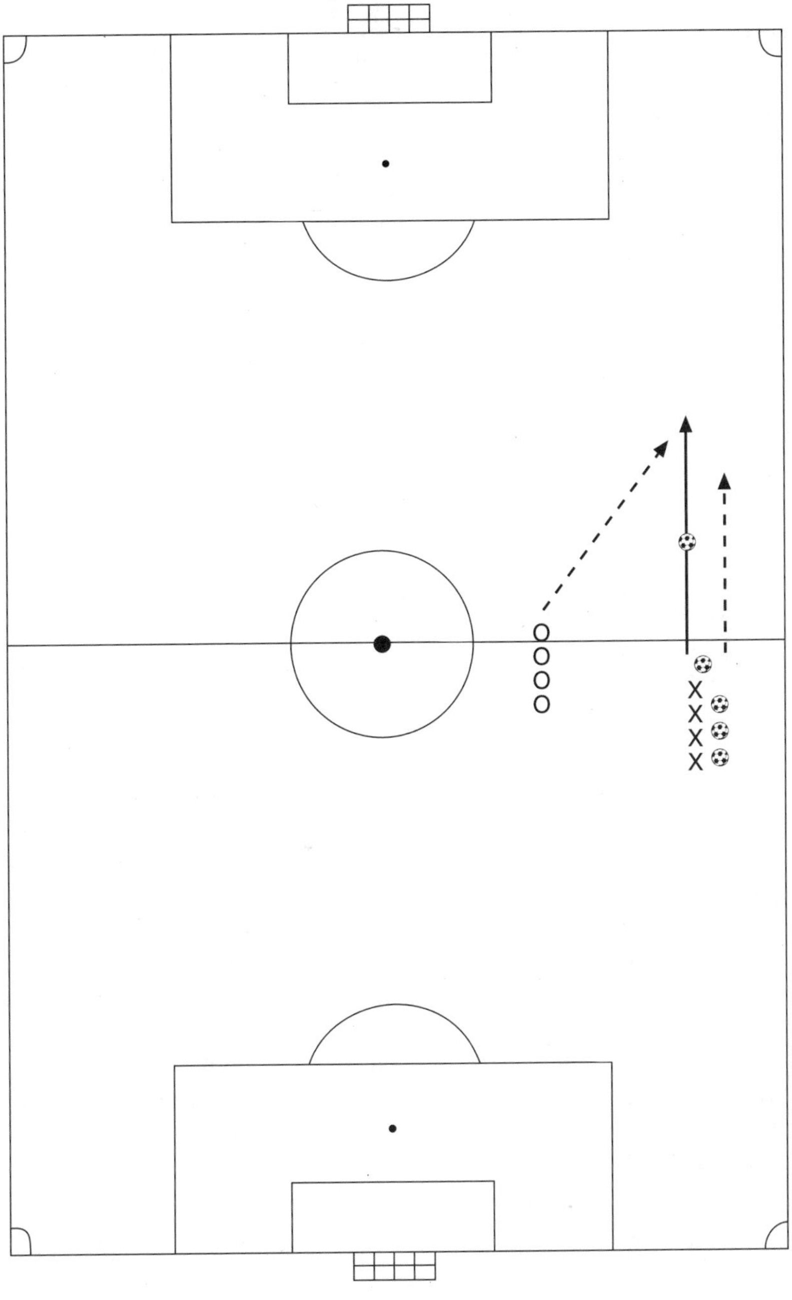

8 Dribbling on the Wing

Purpose

To differentiate dribbling objectives on the wing versus in front of the goal

Organization

Use 6 to 18 players (5 lines, 1 goalkeeper); 1 grid in each corner of the field; 1 line of defenders outside each grid; and 1 line of attackers outside each grid with a supply of balls. A third line of attackers starts outside the penalty area and an additional defender is in front of the goal.

Procedure

1. The offensive player enters the top of the grid with the ball. The defender comes into play at the same time from the corner of the grid.
2. The player with the ball tries to beat the defender and cross the ball into the offensive player (who has entered play from the centerline).
3. Alternate turns with each grid. Have players rotate lines.

Key Points

The difference in this 1 vs. 1 drill is the positioning of the defender and the aim of the dribbler. The defender comes in from the side and tries to force the dribbling player to the sideline. The attacker tries to create enough space to cross the ball into the center.

The dribbler can either advance toward the end line or cut the ball back. The aim is to create enough of an angle to get a cross off. Have attackers try to drive the ball away from the goalkeeper on the crosses. The central attacker should hold the run outside the penalty area until the cross is on. If possible, the crosser and the central attacker should make eye contact before the cross. This will help the attacker time the run to the cross. At the least, the central attacker will have to read the body language of the crosser. The run is made when the ball is in a position to be crossed.

Have the defender pass the ball up the field. The defender has succeeded in part if the dribbler's head is down (looking at the ball and not the rest of the field) or if a bad cross is forced. Defenders should *give away* a corner kick or throw-in only as a last option.

Variations

1. Have the defender be passive at first. Defenders can't tackle the ball; they can only *shepherd* the dribbler and make it difficult for a cross to be played.

2. A server starts play by passing a ball into the corner. The two players race to it. The lines can start closer together, but give the offensive player a few yards head start.
3. Change the position of the cross and the run of the central attacker. Have players try for a far-post cross, for example. Emphasis can also be on the near-post cross.

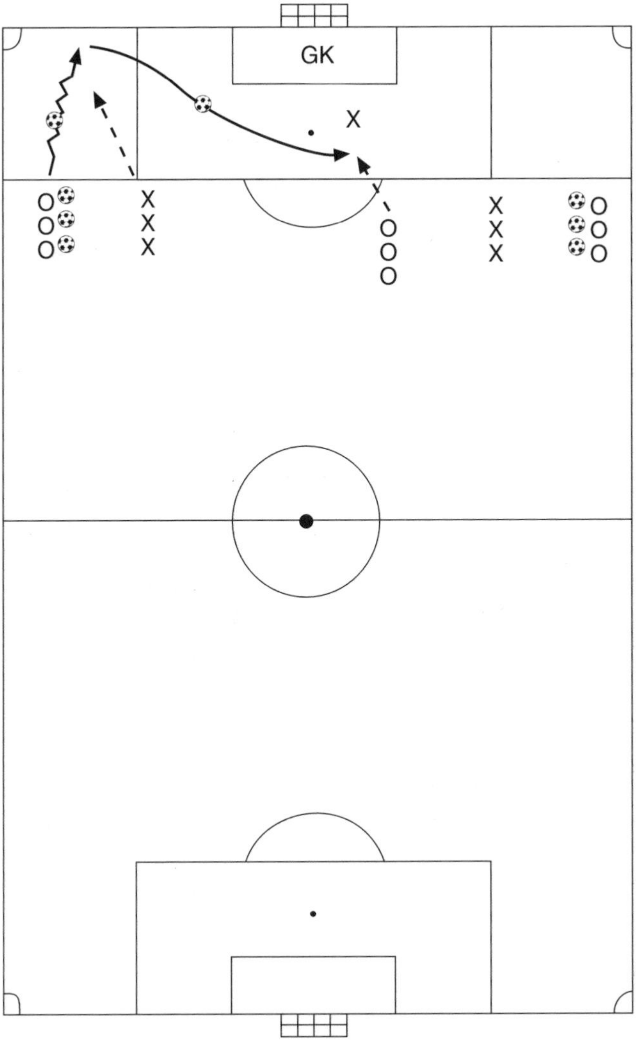

9 Turn and Face

Purpose

To practice controlling the ball, turning with defensive pressure

Organization

Grid 10 by 15 yards; 4 players and 1 ball per grid (have extra balls nearby if available). Position 2 players on opposite ends of the grid; set up the other 2 for a 1 vs. 1 in the grid.

Procedure

1. Play starts with a pass in from a player at the end of the grid.
2. The receiving player tries to control the ball, turn on the defender, and pass the ball to the end-line player on the other end of the grid. The players move back and forth on the line to get open for a pass.
3. If the defender wins the ball, he or she must pass it back to the support player on his or her end of the grid; then play restarts in the other direction. (The defender is now the offensive player.)
4. End-line players switch roles with middle players every two minutes.

Key Points

The defender has the advantage as long as the dribbler's back is to the goal. When the offensive player is able to turn and face the goal, he or she gains the advantage.

Often when the dribbler tries to turn, the defender might attempt to tackle the ball. Quickly moving the ball to the side or *pulling* it away can often beat the tackle. Skilled players can pull the ball backward (create space) and turn at the same time. Then, as the defender is moving in for the tackle, the dribbler pushes the ball forward and accelerates away.

Defenders should be *in the shorts* of the offensive player. They must make it difficult for the offender to turn. If the dribbler can't turn, the ball should be shielded from the defender. Players use upper body strength to hold ground.

The offensive player can create space before the pass by *checking away* from the ball, moving the defender deeper into the grid, then sprinting back to receive the pass. Have players on end lines help teammates by saying "turn" or "no turn" depending on the position of the defender.

Variations

1. Allow no backpasses to the player on the end line.

2. Allow the end-line player who served the ball to enter play, thus creating a 2 vs. 1 situation.
3. Set up two small goals (three yards wide) on each end line. Players score by dribbling through cones (instead of passing to a player).
4. Require players to dribble over the end line to score a point.

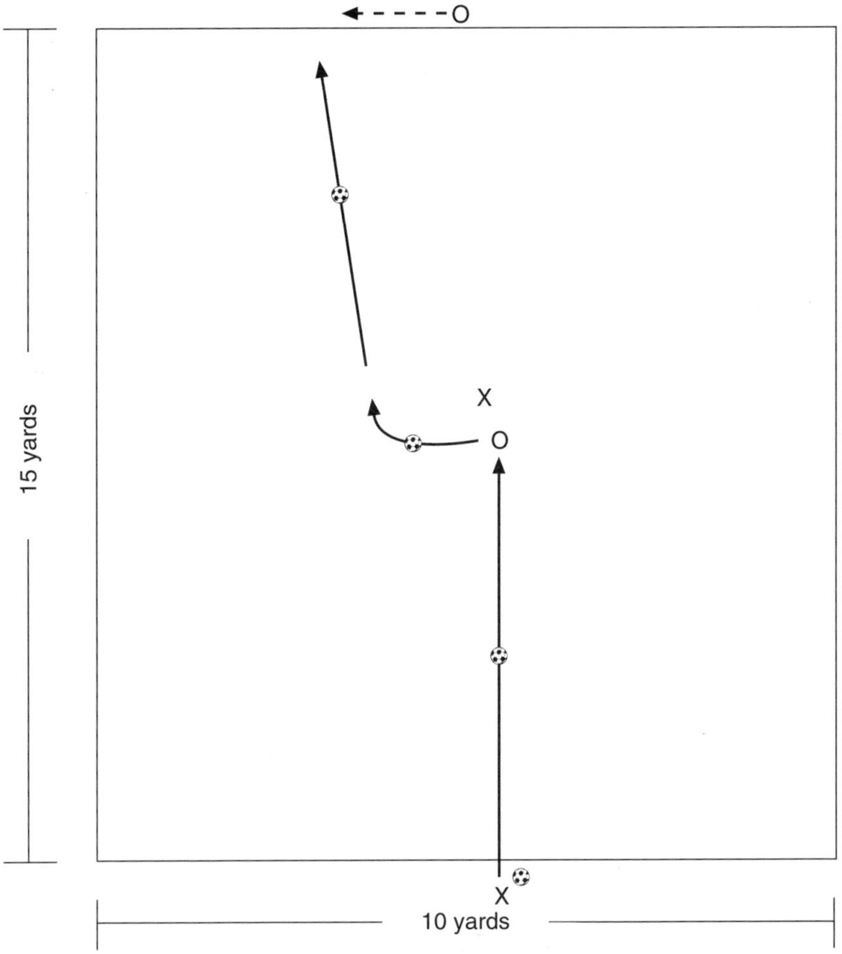

Note: The end-line players change teams depending on the direction of play.

10 Defender's Dilemma

Purpose

To practice running down the through ball, turning the ball away from goal

Organization

Players form 2 lines near midfield. The line of attackers starts 10 yards behind and outside the line of defenders. A server stands to the right of the lines. (Set up duplicate lines on other side of field if lines have more than 5 players each.)

Procedure

1. Two players at the front of each line race to a ball sent toward the end line by the server.
2. Give the defender a slight head start to arrive at the ball first. The objective is for this player to turn the ball away from the goal and pass or dribble it back up the field.
3. If the attacker wins the ball, he or she proceeds to goal.

Key Points

This drill isolates a situation common in games. The defender, running toward his or her goal, is heavily pressured by an attacker from the other team. The defender decides whether to turn the ball and play it up the field or kick it out-of-bounds. A third option is often available if another defender or the goalkeeper is open for a support pass.

As a rule the defender should turn the ball to the outside. Kicking the ball out-of-bounds for a throw-in, or worse, a corner kick is a last option. Skilled players can sometimes turn the ball and deflect it off the legs of the attacker to win possession of the throw-in.

The defender can also let the ball run out-of-bounds if last touched by the other team. This decision is good only if the attacker cannot reach the ball. Often a fake kick is enough to gain the extra time needed for the ball to run out-of-bounds. Note too that the defender can use the body to shield the ball only if the ball is within playing distance.

Variations

1. Change the position of the server.
2. Allow for a pass to the goalkeeper or a sweeper.
3. Have the defender receive the ball closer to the end line.

Defender's Dilemma

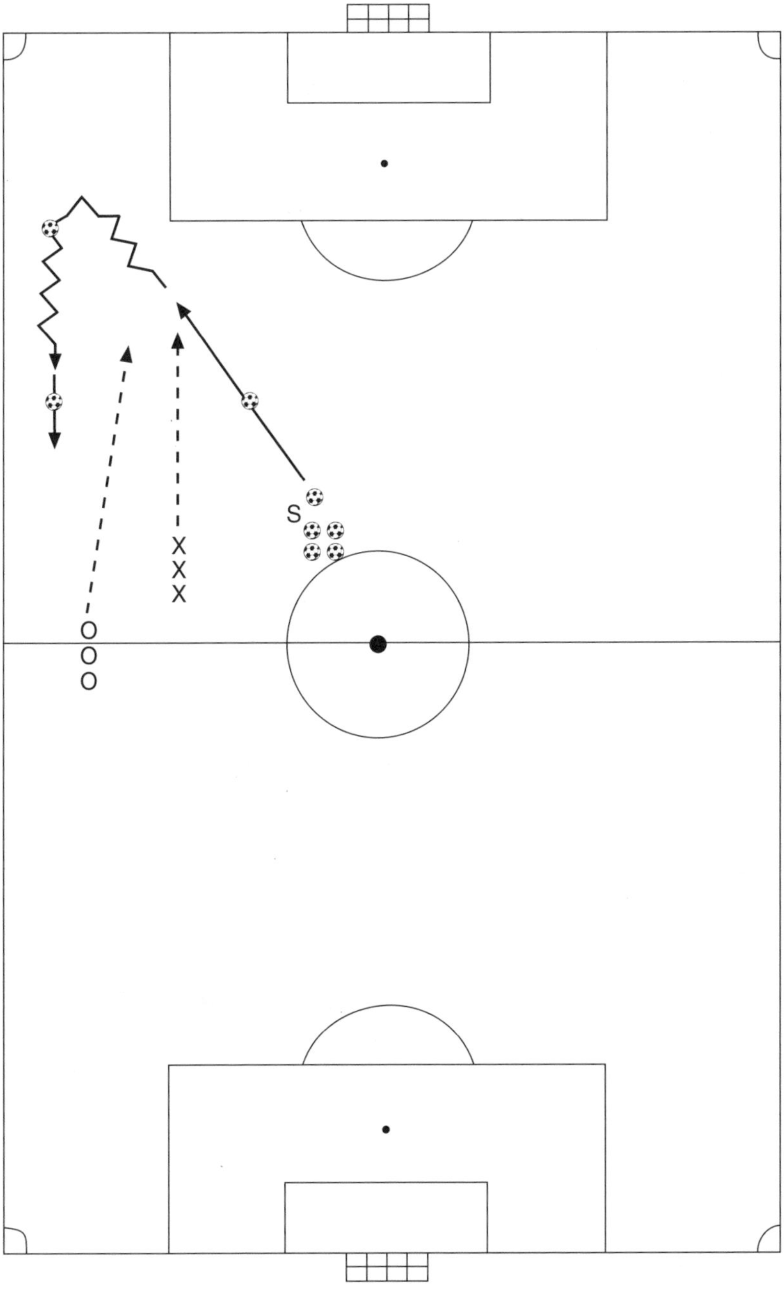

11 Shielding

Purpose

To develop the ability of maintaining possession in a confined space

Organization

Grid 10 by 10 yards, 6 players (2 teams of 3) per grid.

Procedure

1. Each team tries to keep the ball away from the other team in a confined area.
2. A point is scored if the opposite team kicks the ball out of the grid. Restart play by dribbling in from the side.
3. Award the team with possession at the end of a designated time (one minute) three points.
4. Have the losing team sprint three times across the grid.

Key Points

Shielding is a way of retaining possession of the ball against a defender under pressure until a positive move is possible. The body, facing almost sideways, remains between the ball and the opponent. The ball is played with the foot furthest from the defender. It is rolled to either side depending on the position of the defenders.

Players decide how long to hold, when to pass, and what direction to move the ball. The dribbler is in trouble if pinned in a corner or against the side. Supporting teammates will need to make quick runs or perform takeovers to help the player shielding the ball (especially if the player is double teamed).

Variations

1. Allow two players (one from each team) to move on the outside of the grid as support players.
2. Place a small goal or single cone in the center of the grid. Award additional points if a team can hit the target with the ball.
3. Require each player to match up with one other player on the other team. Only matched up players can tackle the ball from each other.

Shielding

10 yards

10 yards

X X X O O O

12 Dribbling to Shoot

Purpose

To recognize and create opportunities for shooting on goal

Organization

Place 2 cones inside the penalty area (alter the position of the cones from time to time). Attackers' line is 35 yards out from goal; servers' line is to the side of the penalty area. A defender starts in the penalty area; a goalkeeper is in the goal.

Procedure

1. The player at the head of the line on the servers' line serves a ball to the first player in the attackers' line. This player dribbles past the defender and shoots on goal.
2. The player who shoots then plays defense against the next player in line. This new defender has to touch either cone before challenging for the ball. (The old defender goes to the end of the servers' line.)
3. It is important that the next ball be served into play moments after the prior shot is taken. (After this pass, the player serving the ball jogs to the end of the attackers' line.)

Key Points

Depending on how you organize the drill (the position of the lines and the cones), players experience different levels of defensive pressure while setting up for a shot. In any case, the player must settle the ball and advance to goal. The defender might challenge from straight on or come in from the side.

The dribbler maximizes time and space by heading straight to the penalty area. The player should take a shot at the first opportunity. Have players work on placement. The shot must be on target. The opportunity cannot be wasted.

Variations

1. Alter the position of the cones.
2. Require defender to touch both cones.
3. Have the server play defense (1 vs. 2).
4. Require the defender to touch the near cone and the dribbler to go outside the far cone (or vice versa).
5. Start play with a chip pass or throw-in.

Dribbling to Shoot

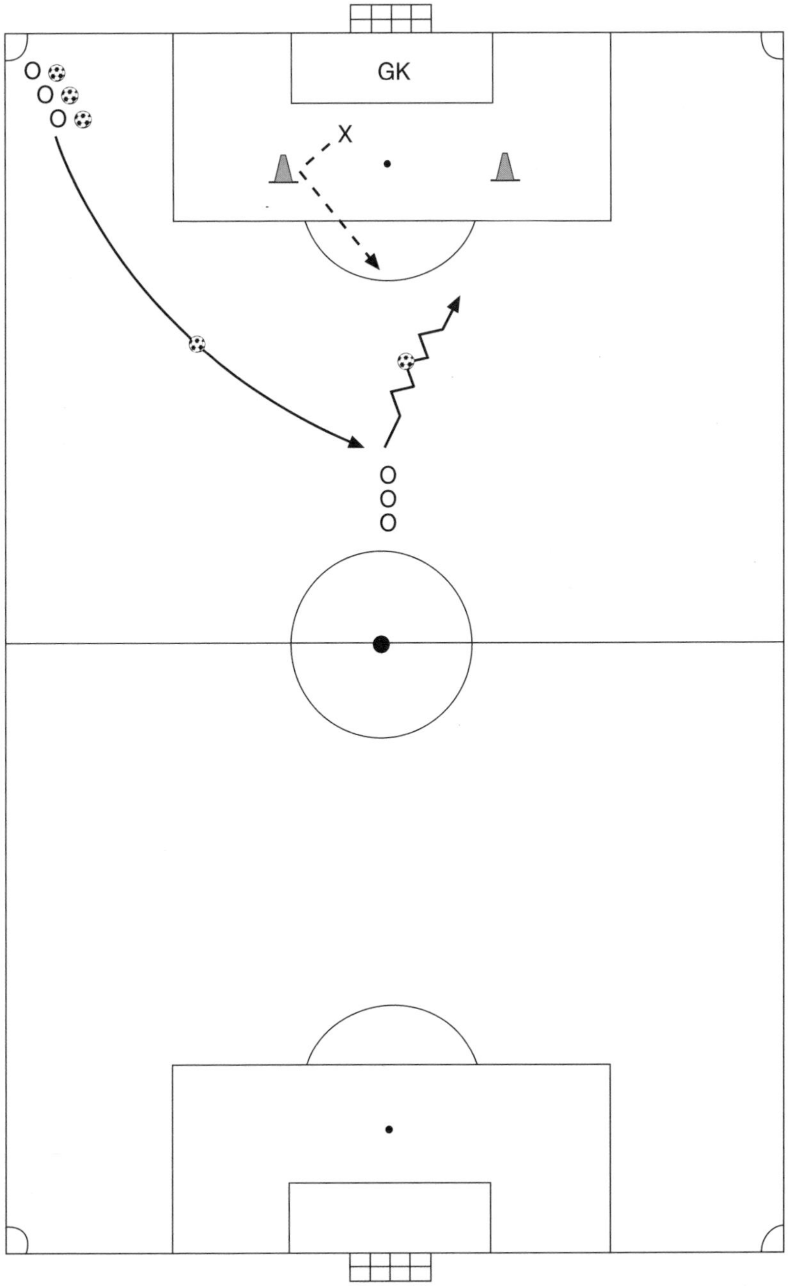

13 Dribbling Against the Goalkeeper

Purpose

To focus on finishing the breakaway

Organization

Position 1 line 30 yards out from goal; 2 goalkeepers take turns inside the goal.

Procedure

1. The player at the front of the line dribbles toward goal and tries to score.
2. The goalkeeper starts on the line and can advance toward the ball at any time.

Key Points

Players should dribble straight to the goal. If the goalkeeper charges, the offensive player should dribble around the goalkeeper then shoot on goal. The trick will be to force the goalkeeper to dive or slide in one direction then to quickly push or cut the ball in the other. This is a good dribbling exercise in that it exaggerates what it takes to commit a defender.

If the goalkeeper charges then stops, a shot may be available by lofting the ball over or by directing it to the side. If the goalkeeper stays on the line, the dribbler should proceed until scoring is an extremely likely outcome.

Variations

1. Have player receive a pass then dribble toward goal. Change the position of the server and the type of pass delivered.
2. Put a time limit in effect for the player to take a shot (five seconds).

Dribbling Against the Goalkeeper

GK

O
O
O
O

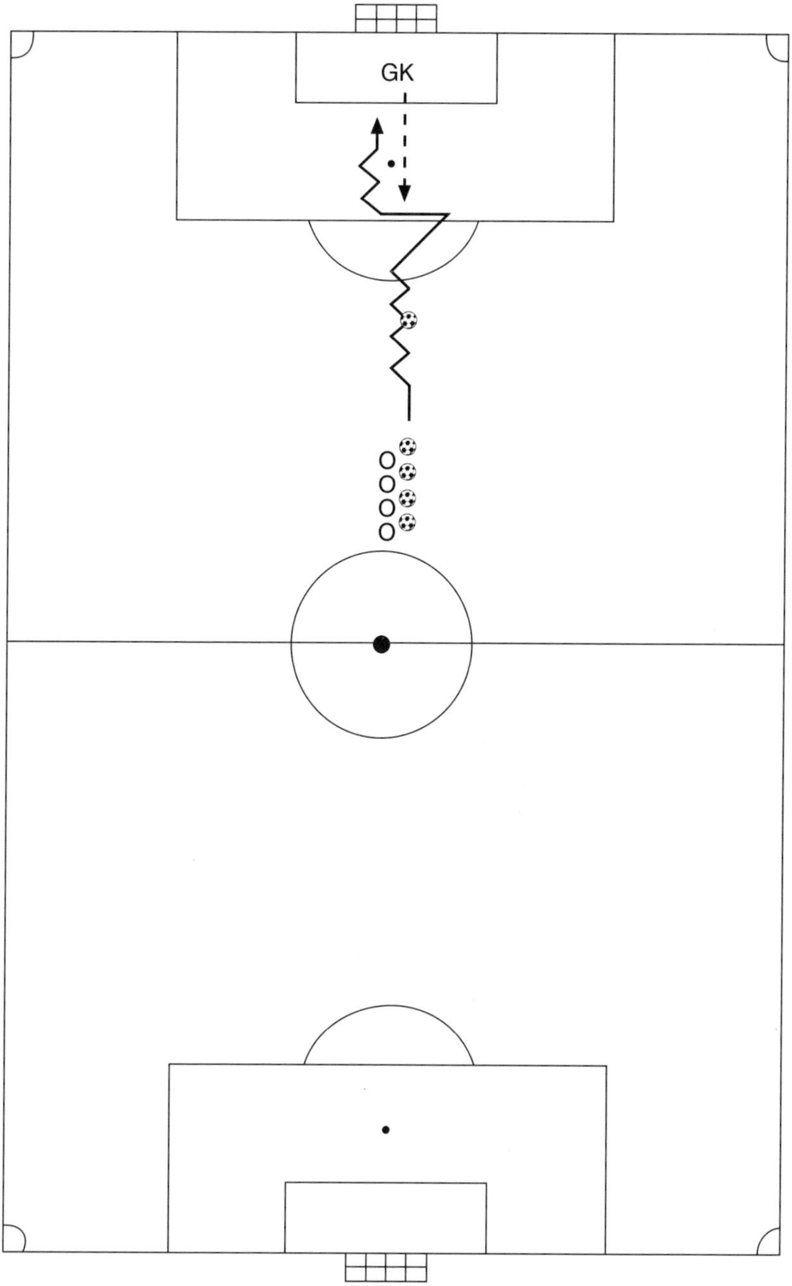

14 1 vs. 1 Challenge

Purpose

To practice and test 1 vs. 1 skills

Organization

Grid 15 by 20 yards; 2 players stand shoulder to shoulder between a pair of goals 5 yards apart inside the grid. Goals are 2 yards wide. Place 1 ball 5 yards in front of the players. Set up 1 grid per pair of players.

Procedure

1. At the signal, players race to the ball and try to win possession. Either player can score at either goal from either direction.
2. The player with possession continues to score as many goals as possible until the opponent gains possession (then the opponent tries to score).
3. Play continues nonstop for one minute. Allow no ties. Players keep playing until someone scores a goal (sudden death).
4. The winners advance to the next grid; losers go back one. Give a three-minute rest period before the next round. Keep track of wins and losses.*

Key Points

This exercise incorporates a variety of skills for winning 1 vs. 1 situations including speed, strength, and ball control. The drill also measures a player's mental attitude. Are players competitive? What happens when they lose?

Stamina and fitness are important if players are required to perform this drill repeatedly.

Variation

You can incorporate this activity into *ladder training* by creating as many grids as there are pairs of players. After each competition the winner moves up a grid, the loser goes down. (Note that players at the first and last grid might have to sit out a round.)

*See chapter 6 on the 1 vs. 1 challenge for ideas on how to keep score and how to use this game for player selection (tryouts).

1 vs. 1 Challenge

20 yards

O X

15 yards

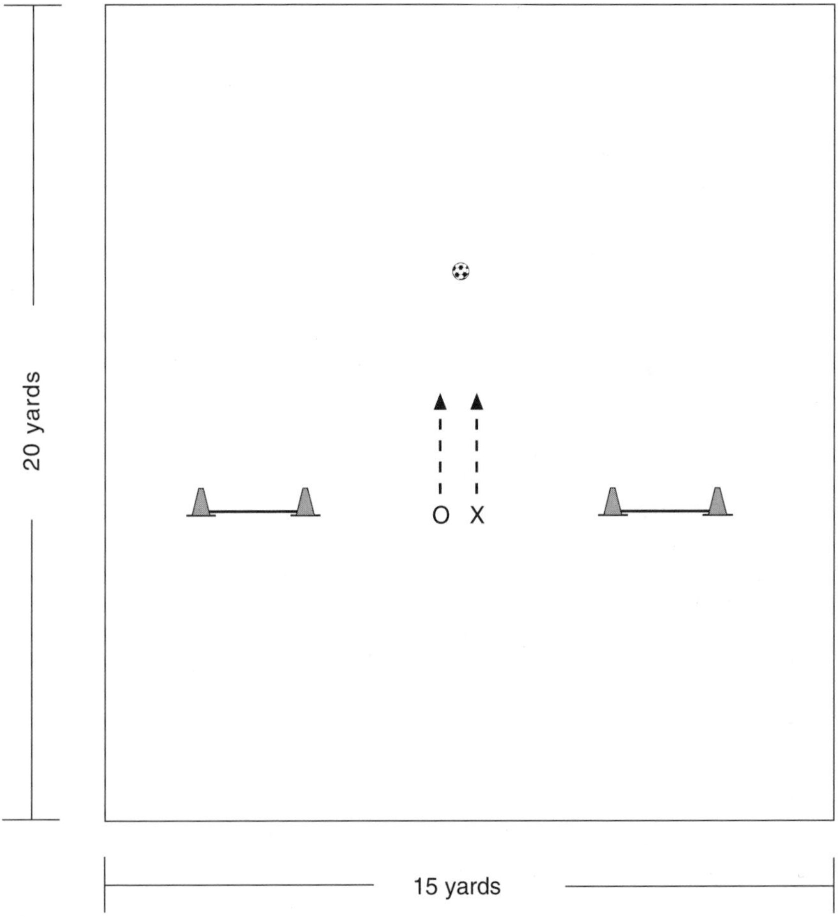

15 Dribbling Inside the Defender

Purpose

To practice dribbling inside the defender, defensive shepherding

Organization

A line of attackers with a supply of balls starts near the midfield line (about 5 yards in from the sideline). Set up a line of 6 cones diagonally across the field (starting from the touchline and angling back toward the center of the field). Each opening between cones represents a gate. A defender starts even with the last cone.

Procedure

1. The first player in line tries to dribble past the defender and through a gate. Award points according to which gate the dribbler passes through. Gate 5 is worth five points. Gate 4 is worth four points and so on. Gate 5, the gate closest to the center of the field, is the primary target for the dribbler.
2. The defender tries to shepherd the player to the outside and win the ball.
3. One point is awarded to the defender if the dribbler loses the ball or doesn't make it through any gate.
4. Play continues until the attacker shoots on goal or the defender wins the ball. No points are awarded if a shot is not taken.
5. After dribbling, the player takes a turn as a defender. (The defender goes to the end of the attacking line.)

Key Points

This exercise illustrates the importance of turning the ball inside toward the goal. The sooner a player can accomplish the task, the more points the effort is worth. Defenders try to deny central penetration by overplaying to the inside. They *give* the dribbler room to advance down the line.

You might stress that the offensive player has to maintain possession of the ball after passing through the gate for the point to count. The defender tries to win the ball until a shot is taken.

Variations

1. Alter the angle of the cones. Place them in a straight line parallel to the end line (10 to 15 yards from the end line).
2. Change the starting position of the dribbler relative to the defender. Have the dribbler start even with defender, for example. Also try the defender starting inside the dribbler, then the defender positioned outside the dribbler.

Dribbling Inside the Defender

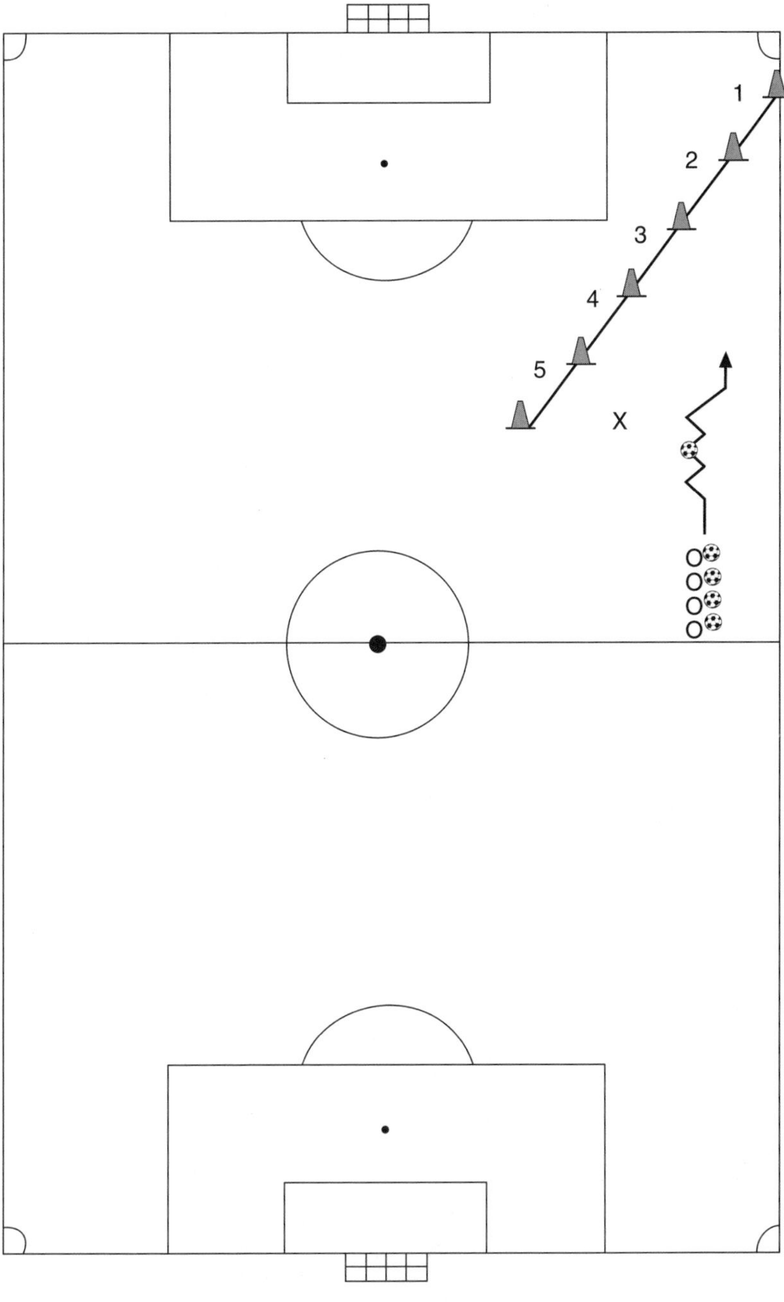

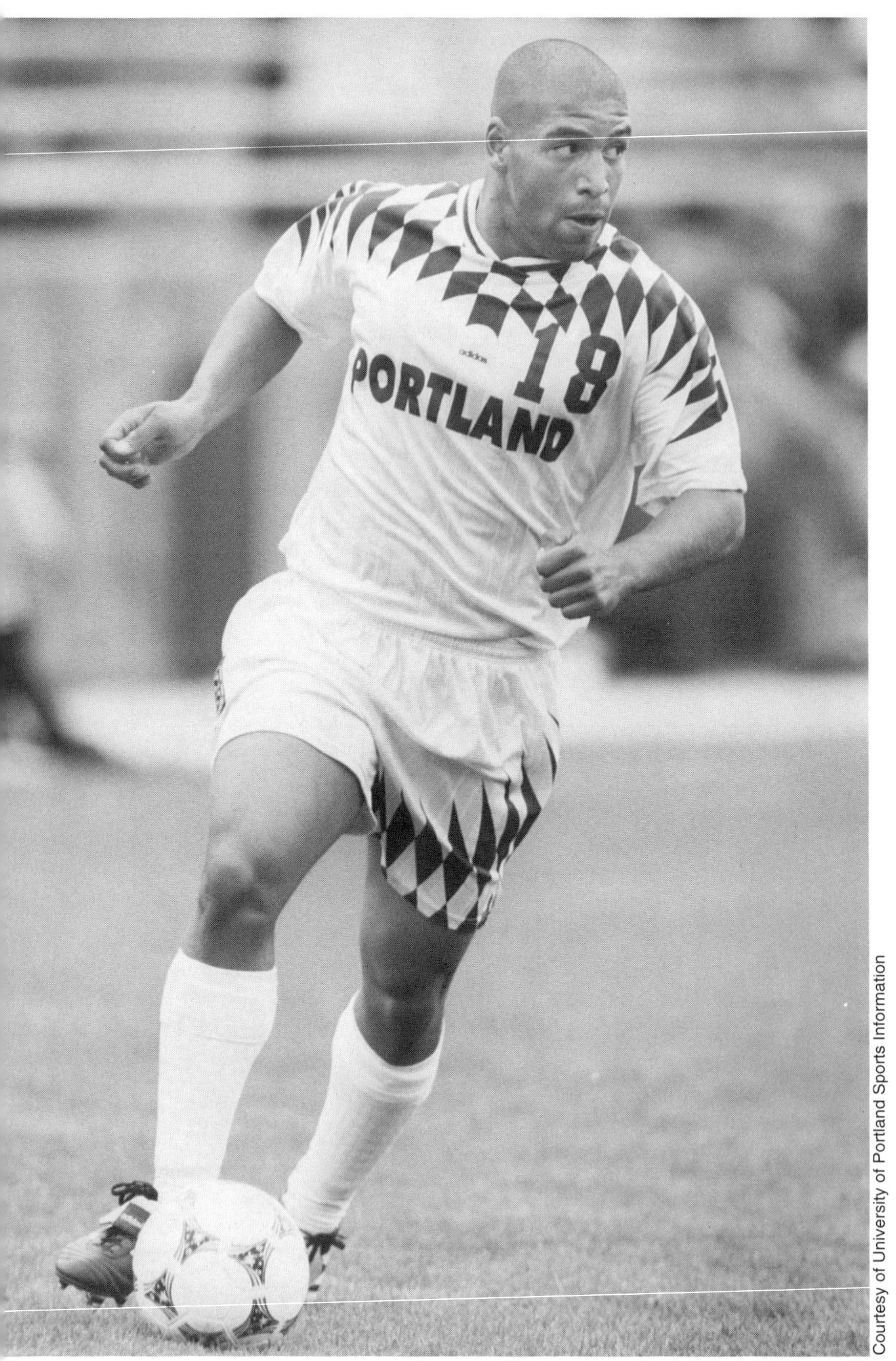

Courtesy of University of Portland Sports Information

CHAPTER 2

Improving Vision & Decision Making

The previous chapter focused on a player dribbling around a defender. In this chapter the emphasis is on deciding whether to dribble or pass. The chapter could have been called See and Choose because the ability to see the field and choose the best course of play separates skilled players from the rest of the pack.

Improving field vision is a crucial part of training in competitive soccer programs. Good vision becomes habitual. It develops over time as players become more comfortable with the ball and more apt at handling defensive pressure. Whereas a young, inexperienced player might control the ball first then assess his or her options, the skilled player sees his or her options before the ball arrives.

The better the vision, the more options a player can see. The drills in this chapter ask players to identify the degree of defensive pressure, the space available to dribble or pass, and the position of teammates. These are the key factors that determine the players' options.

Once players evaluate the options they are asked to decide what to do. In this chapter, emphasis has been given to isolated decisions. The drills are in large part variations of 2 vs. 2 or 2 vs. 1 situations. Players will decide when to pass (if at all) in a variety of situations. Likewise, supporting teammates have to decide where to run and when. Improving vision should be stressed in even simple passing exercises. Always look for opportunities to encourage players to glance over their shoulders or to the sides before receiving the ball.

Finally, it should be emphasized, the more comfortable a player is with a ball performing the routine tasks, the easier it will be to look up and see the field. In this sense, technique, particularly ball control, is a prerequisite for vision training. Skilled players are always working hard to improve the ease at which they receive and control the ball.

Find the Space

Purpose

To practice dribbling, passing, and communicating with teammates

Organization

All players move freely on half the field. Put 2 balls in play.

Procedure

1. At first, players run in and out of space interpassing two balls with no more than two touches per player.
2. Progress through the following: pass one touch; add a defender; add two defenders.
3. If a ball leaves the playing area or is won by a defender require the whole team to do 10 push-ups or equivalent.

Key Points

Players practice passing and moving in this drill. They have to be aware of activity in 360 degrees as they look for space, passing options, and other players. Good communication is also crucial. Players should make eye contact before passing the ball. After players pass a ball away, they should immediately look for the second ball.

Variations

1. Let the goalkeepers play defense by trying to intercept or catch the ball with their hands.
2. To emphasize dribbling, give every player a ball and have three defenders trying to win possession. If a ball is taken away, the players switch roles. (Defenders cannot win possession by kicking the ball out-of-bounds.)
3. Make the space smaller.

Find the Space

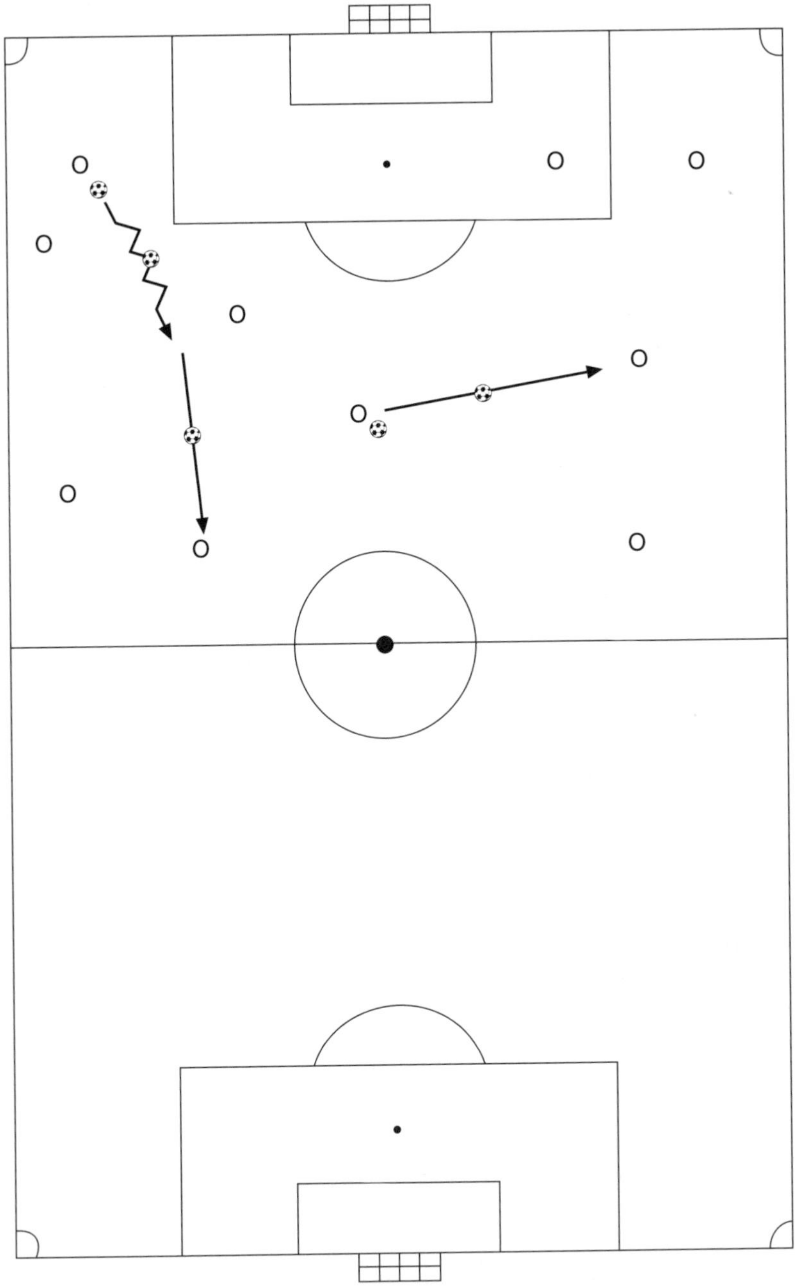

17 Pinball Warm-Up

Purpose

To practice anticipating passing angles

Organization

Use 5 players; position 4 inside the penalty area and assign them a number 1 through 4. Position the fifth player (with the ball) outside the area.

Procedure

1. The four players without balls jog back and forth across the width of the penalty area.
2. The player with the ball completes passes to the jogging players in consecutive numeric progression: pass to player O_1, then to player O_2, then to player O_3, and so on. After receiving the ball, the jogging player passes the ball back to the player outside the penalty area.
3. Limit all players to a maximum of two touches.
4. Incorporate variations to increase the difficulty of this exercise.

Key Points

This exercise forces player O_1 to look up and identify the appropriate next pass before the ball is received. The fifth player should be up on the balls of the feet. As the ball is passed to this player, watch his or her eyes. Do they follow the ball? Do they look up the field to assess the position of the next player?

Also pay attention to the weight of the pass. Does the jogging player have to break stride to gather the ball? Is the pass easy to one or two touch back?

Variations

1. Have the target player move freely in the area with the other players.
2. Require one-touch passes.
3. Allow no verbal communication.
4. After completing pass, the numbered player sprints behind the goal and reenters play.
5. Jogging players interpass a second ball while drill proceeds.

Pinball Warm-Up

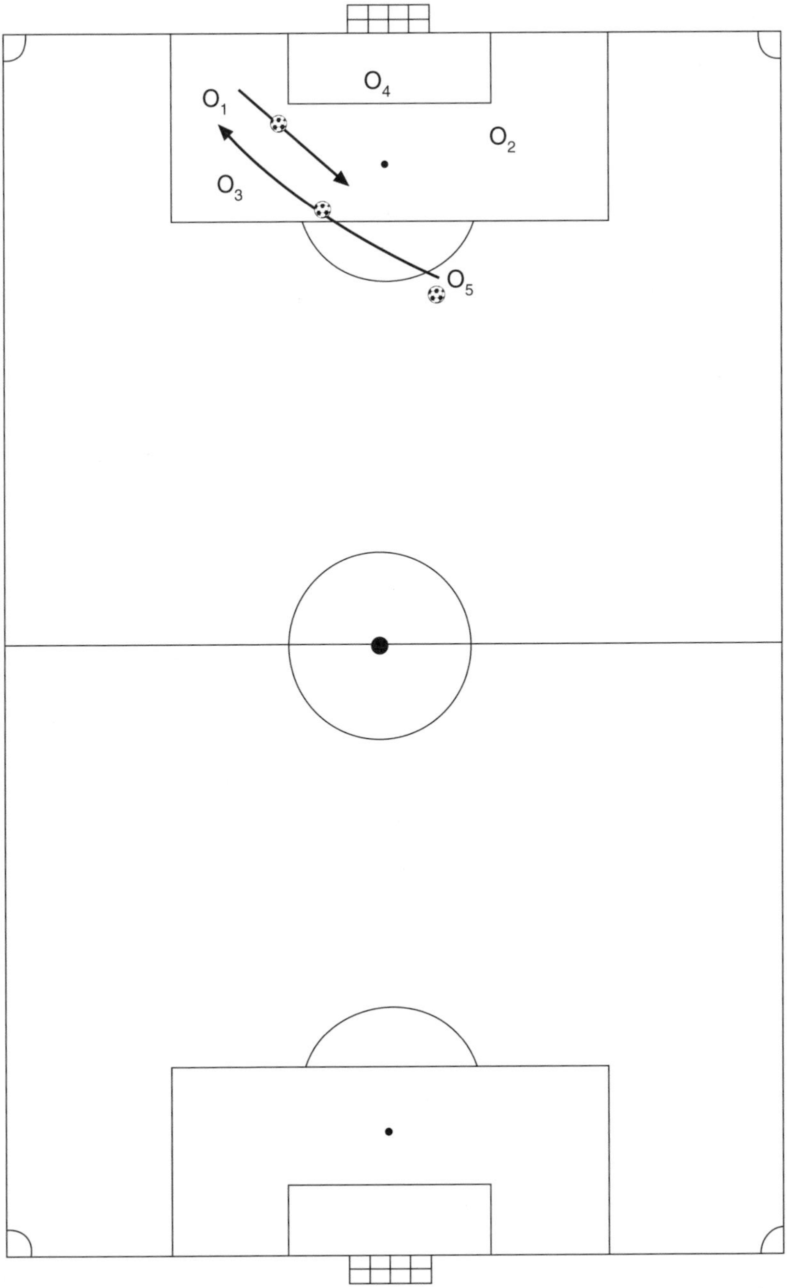

18 4 vs. 1 One-Touch Passing

Purpose

To practice one-touch passing with slight defensive pressure

Organization

Use 6 to 10 players; position 4 at the corners of a square 5 to 7 yards per side with 1 defender in the middle. The remaining players line up outside the square.

Procedure

1. The four offensive players in the square play keep-away from the defender.
2. Players must pass the ball away with a one-touch pass.
3. If an offensive player makes a mistake and the ball leaves the grid or the defender wins possession, then the player leaves the grid and goes to the end of the line. The defender takes the open spot in the corner, and the first person in line becomes the new defender.

Key Points

One-touch soccer, as used in this drill or as a restriction in other drills or scrimmages, is one of the best methods to force players to *see* the field. Because a player has only one chance to get off a successful pass, he or she must know where the intended target is before the ball arrives. This drill also forces players to pay attention to the weight of the pass.

Variations

1. Have players use two touches.
2. Play 3 vs. 1 or 5 vs. 2.
3. Change the size of the grid.

4 vs. 1 One-Touch Passing

18

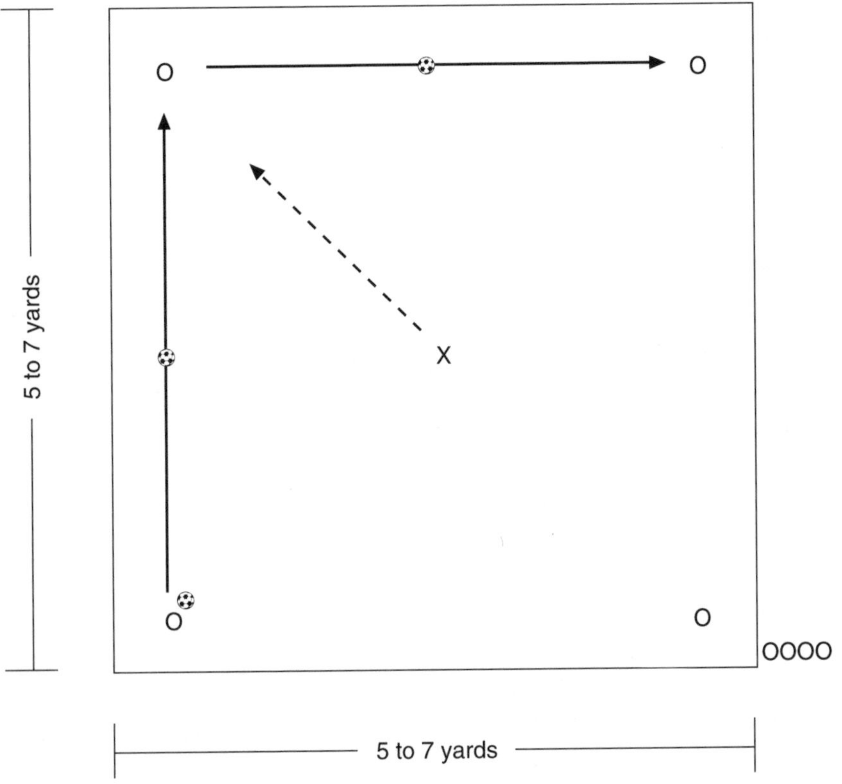

19 Two-Player Passing Combinations

Purpose

To practice timing passes and runs for 2 vs. 1 situations

Organization

Use 3 lines, 1 goalkeeper. As seen in *a*, position 1 line of defenders on the end line to the side of goal and 2 lines of attackers near the midfield line. The defenders start with the balls.

Procedure

1. The defender at the front of the line starts play by passing the ball to either attacker at the front of the lines.
2. The player receiving the ball controls the ball and dribbles toward the defender. This attacker can proceed to goal or pass to the teammate.
3. After a shot on goal or after the defender wins the ball, have players rotate lines.

Key Points

The dribbler should aim to commit the defender before passing the ball. Doing so creates an opportunity for the second attacker. The second attacker has to read when the pass is on and make the run accordingly. Timing is critical. If the second attacker *shows* too soon the defender can cover both players. If the run for the pass comes too late, the dribbler might not be able to pass or the defender will have time to recover.

Variation

Start with one line of attackers and one defender. The first player in line moves out 10 yards in front of the line and is marked by a defender (goal-side), as illustrated in *b*. The next player in line starts play by passing the ball forward. A return pass off to the side can often beat the defender. If the defender *cheats* to one side or plays the pass, the offensive player should keep the ball and turn it into space.

Two-Player Passing Combinations

a

b

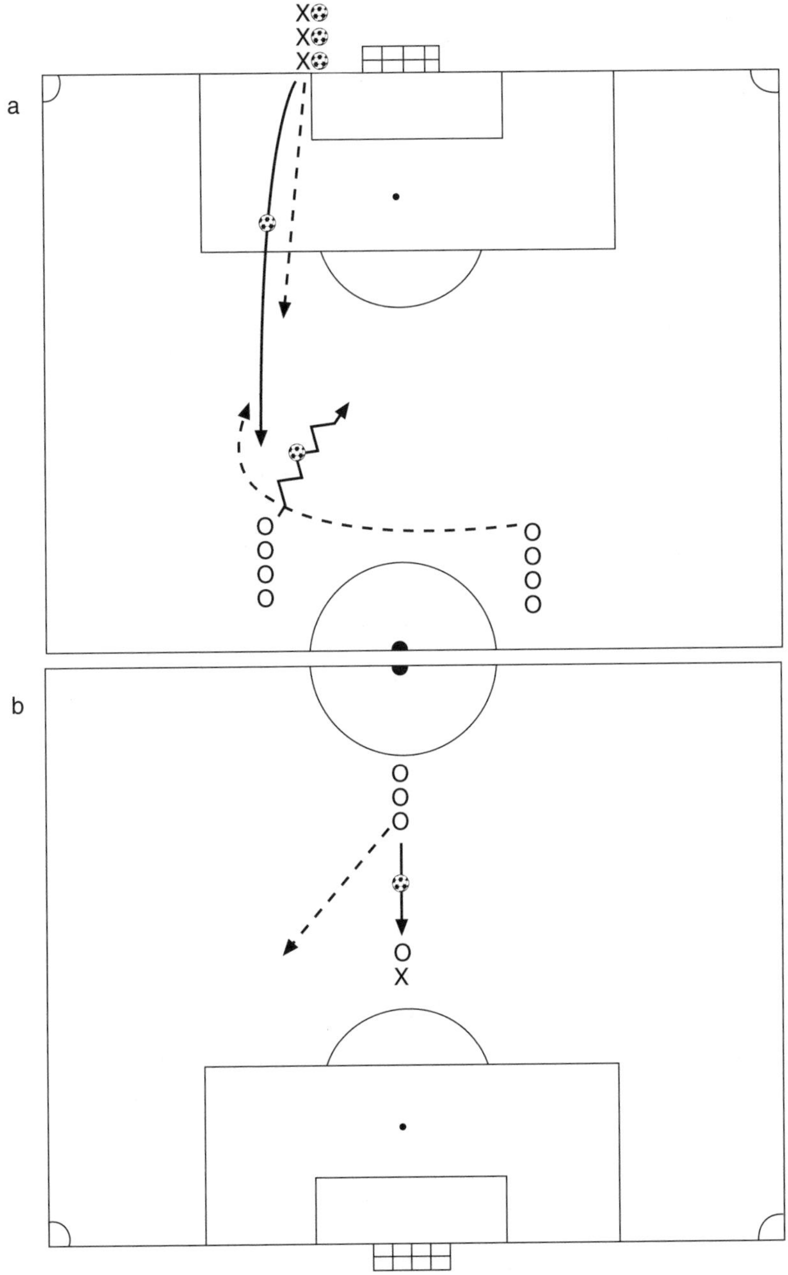

20 Dribbling Inside Versus Outside

Purpose

To distinguish between the decision of dribbling to the inside or outside of the defender

Organization

Form 2 lines near the midfield line. A goalkeeper is in the goal. The player at the head of 1 line has the ball. The defender (the first person from the other line) starts halfway between the ball and the goal.

Procedure

1. The player with the ball has to dribble at the defender. The second attacker enters play several seconds after the first player starts dribbling.
2. If the defender is beaten on the outside, the player dribbling the ball tries to cross it to the second attacker, who runs into play accordingly.
3. If dribbler is able to penetrate the defender on the inside, the second attacker makes an overlap to the outside.
4. The dribbling player becomes the defender for the next player in line. The other players return to the end of the line.

Key Points

Instruct dribbler to take the ball at the defender. As the space closes, the dribbler will have to change speed and direction. The body swerve is perhaps the simplest and most effective method of unbalancing an opponent. Feint to the left, for example, by dipping the shoulder to the left and planting the left foot, then as the defender moves in the dribbler has an opportunity to accelerate away to the right.

Timing is the key to success. Fake too early, and the defender has time to recover. Fake too late, and the defender has a better chance at the ball.

The defender has been somewhat successful if the dribbler is forced to the outside.

Variation

Add another defender who starts on the goalpost. Allow this defender to enter play only if the ball is passed to the second offensive player.

Dribbling Inside Versus Outside

GK

X

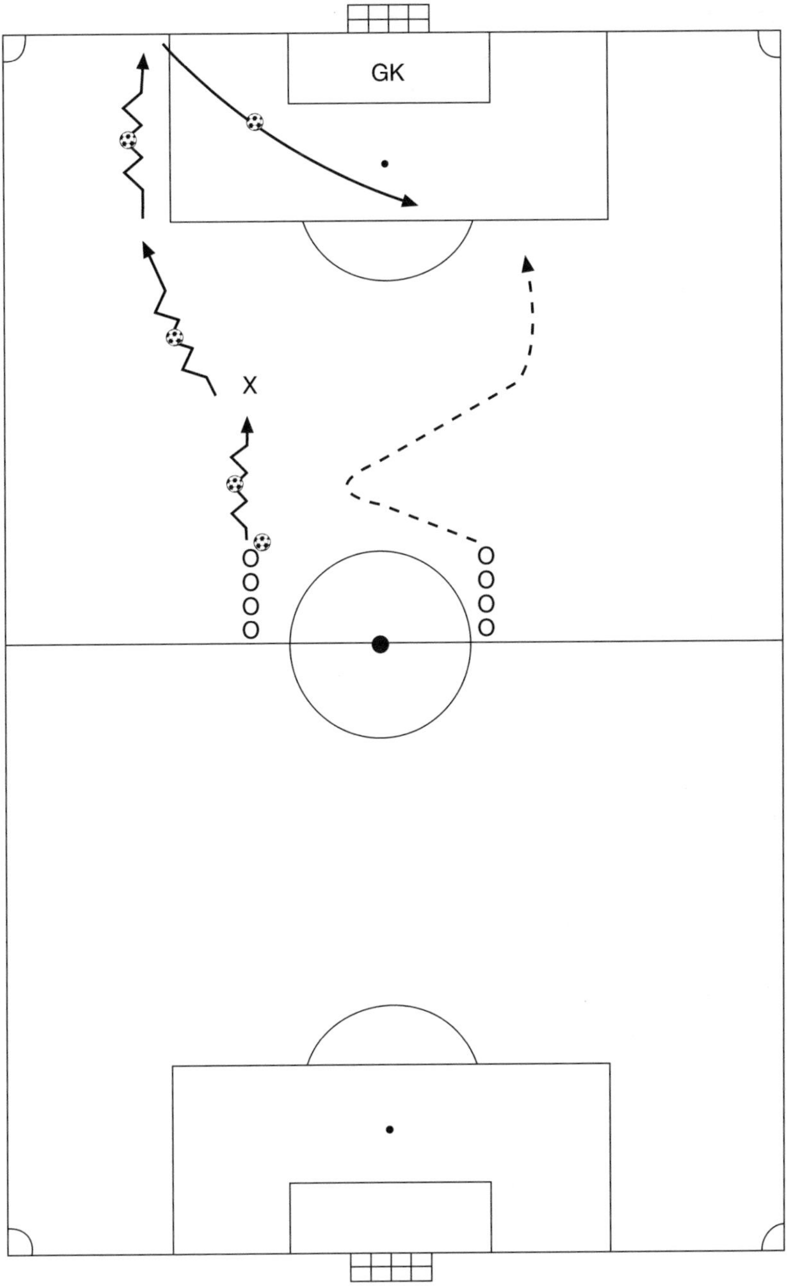

21 Double Teamed

Purpose

To practice recognizing when not to dribble ahead to goal

Organization

Form 1 line near midfield. Use 2 defenders, a keeper in the goal, and 1 server with a supply of balls.

Procedure

1. Player O_1 at the front of the line receives a pass from the server and dribbles at the first defender X_1.
2. The second player in line, O_2, enters play as the second attacker two or three seconds later.
3. The two offensive players pass or dribble depending on the position of the defenders and try to advance the ball for a shot on goal.
4. If defenders win the ball before a shot or cross, they should play it back to the server.
5. Switch defenders after three or four turns.

Key Points

If a player has a 1 vs. 1, encourage him or her to go for goal. The position of the second defender determines whether the dribble is on. If the dribbling player can beat one defender and shoot, then encourage the dribble. If the second defender is in a good support position and ready to pressure the dribbler (should the first defender fail), then the best decision is a pass.

Instruct the first defender to overplay the middle of the field, shielding the dribbler toward the sideline. If the second defender provides close support, the first defender can go ahead with the tackle.

The second attacker is the key to the offense. The timing and direction of the run will determine the position of the second defender. The second defender should not be able to provide support for the first defender and cover the run of the second attacker.

Variation

Have the second offensive player and the second defensive player enter play from the endline.

Double Teamed

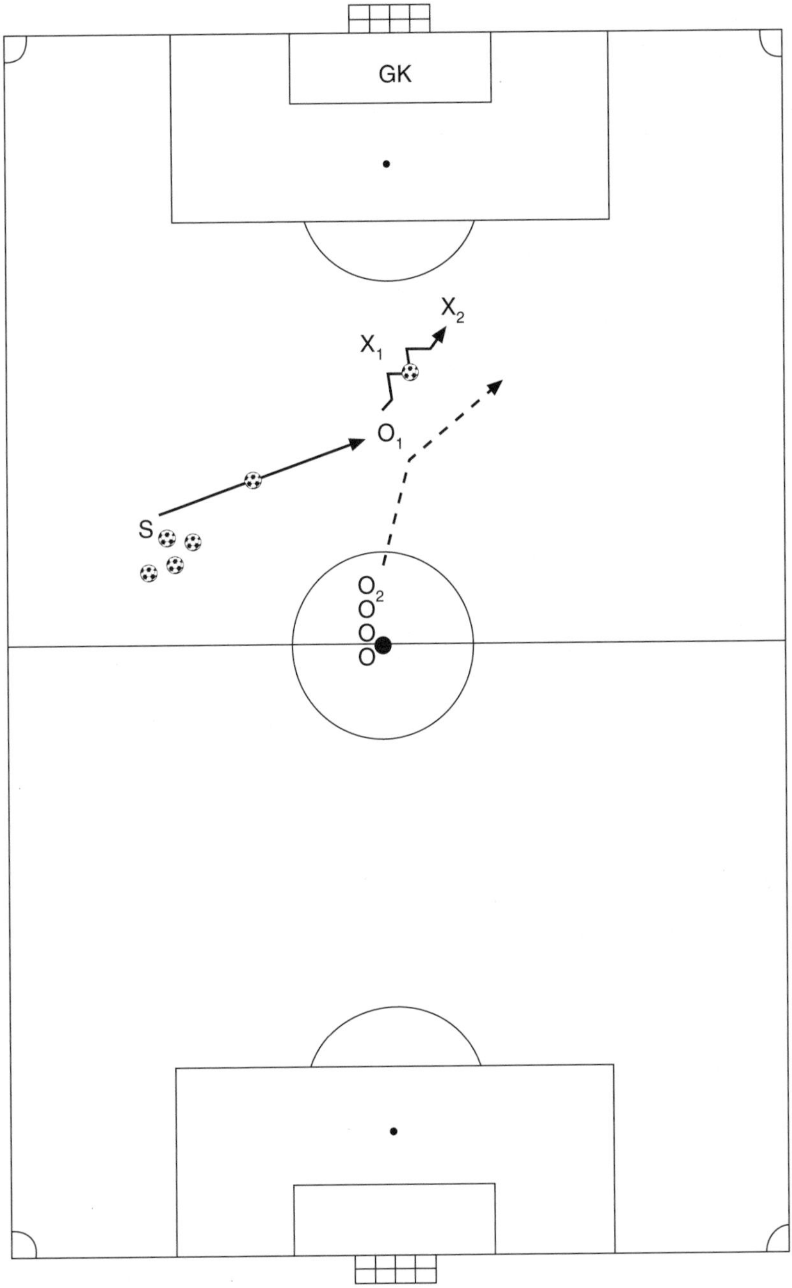

Sequential Passing (5 vs. 1)

Purpose

To practice anticipating passing angles, moving off the ball

Organization

Square grid 10 to 12 yards on a side; 6 players (5 offense, 1 defense) with 1 ball inside the grid. Give each offensive player a number 1 through 5.

Procedure

1. Five players play keep-away from one defender while passing in sequential order: player O_1 passes to player O_2, player O_2 to player O_3, and so on (O_5 passes to O_1).
2. Switch defenders after one or two minutes.

Key Points

Each player needs to anticipate where to be to receive a pass when his or her turn comes up. Anticipation of the proper position is necessary if a one-touch or two-touch restriction is in effect.

When players are not involved in a pass, encourage them to stay wide in the grid (shuffle around the perimeter). This will create space for the others and allow a good view of the playing area. When players sprint into their space have them adjust by moving. A balanced grid with players evenly spread out should result.

Have players *play to feet* when possible. Receiving players should easily reach and control passes. The player receiving the ball should know where the next player is before the ball arrives.

Variations

1. Play with a passive defender until a flow is established.
2. Increase the size of the grid.
3. Once player O_5 is reached, pass in reverse order (1-2-3-4-5-4-3-2-1-2- and so on).
4. Add another defender.
5. Limit the number of touches to one or two per player.

Sequential Passing (5 vs. 1)

O_1 O_3

X

O_5

O_2

O_4

10 to 12 yards

10 to 12 yards

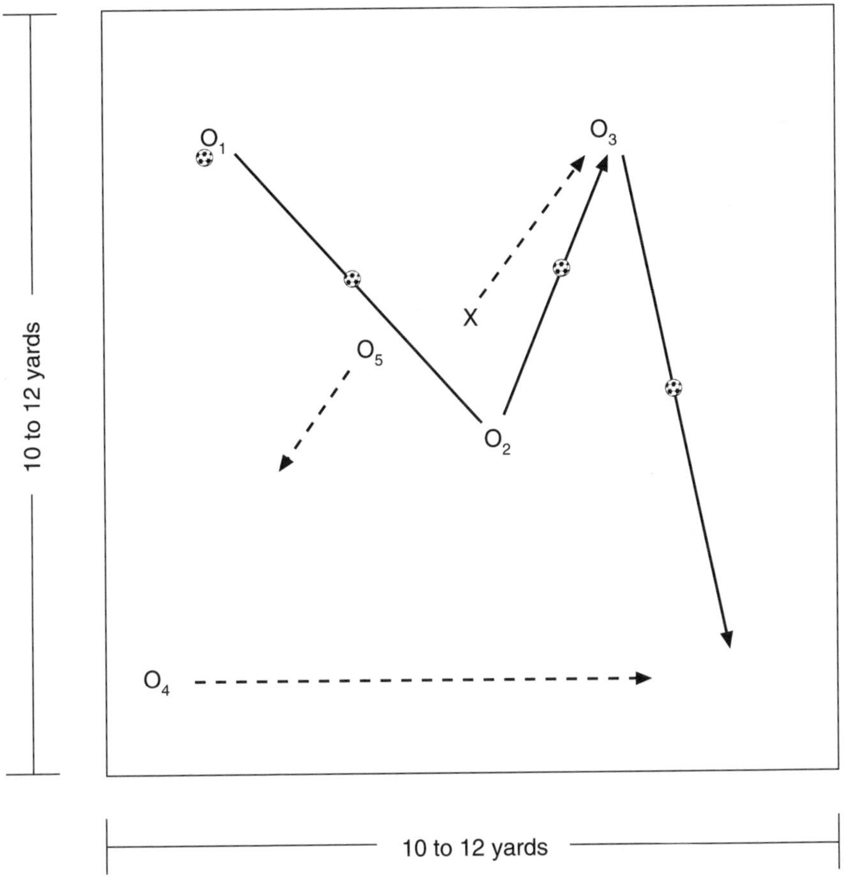

23 Across the Grid

Purpose

To develop the habit of assessing the field before receiving the ball

Organization

Grid 5 to 7 yards by 10 to 15 yards; 4 players per grid, 1 offensive player on each end line, 1 offensive and 1 defensive player in middle of grid, 1 ball.

Procedure

1. Three players work together to advance the ball from one side of the grid to the other. End players can pass directly across the grid to each other or they can link a pass with the middle player. The middle player can dribble or backpass.
2. Rotate defenders after two minutes.

Key Points

Because the end players are allowed to pass directly to each other, the defender always has to pay attention to two passing lanes. This allows the middle player to play off the concerns of the defender. In other words, the defender can't just follow the player in the middle. Have the offensive player make checking runs to the ball on an angle. This will open the grid for a pass or it will create space to receive a pass and turn with the ball.

Variations

1. Allow the player on the end line to enter the grid after passing the ball.
2. Make the grid narrower (or wider).
3. Allow passes on the ground only.
4. Implement a five-second rule: Players must play the ball within five seconds of receiving it.
5. Allow the middle player to dribble the ball across the opposite end line (for a point).

Across the Grid

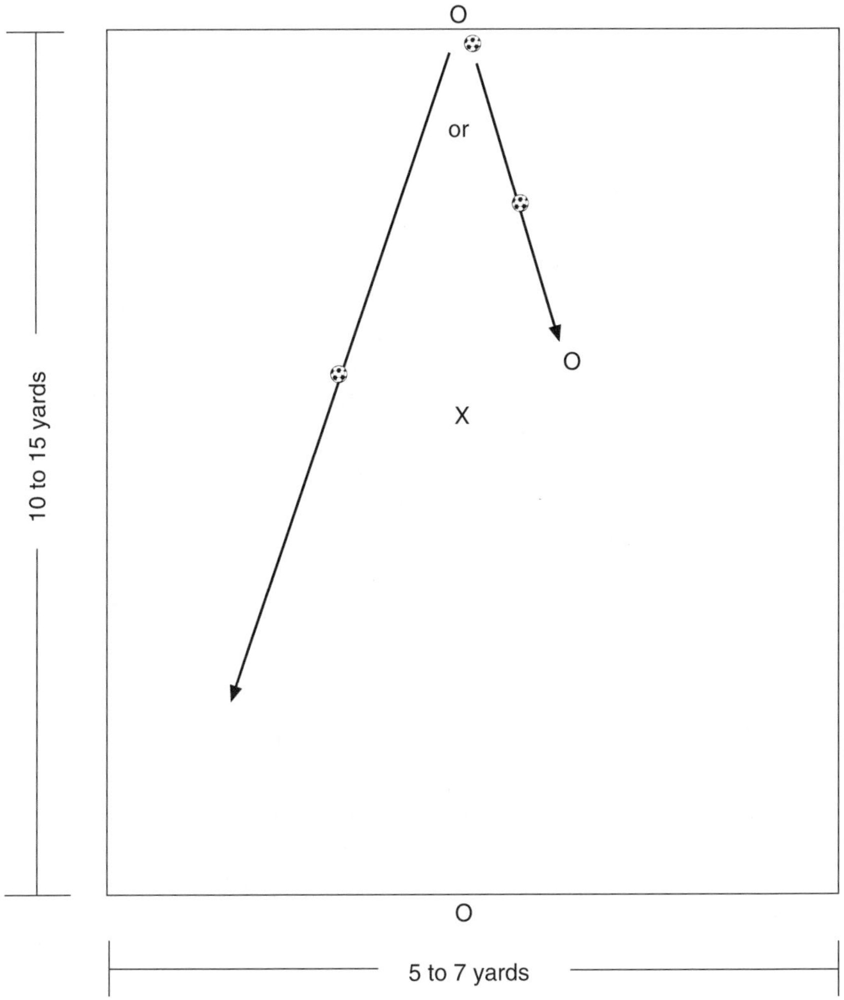

24 Possession or Punishment

Purpose

To practice maintaining possession with short passes and with an eye to the long pass

Organization

Set up 2 grids side by side, 15 by 15 yards each. Use 12 players (3 teams of 4); 2 teams are offense (Os and Zs). Each of these teams stays in 1 grid. The third team (Xs) plays defense. Assign 2 defenders to each grid.

Procedure

1. One of the offensive teams plays keep-away against the defenders in one grid (4 vs. 2). After these players complete three passes, they try to advance the ball to the other grid. The first pass into the grid cannot be challenged by a defender (first pass is free). The four offensive players in this grid now try to complete three passes and play continues.
2. If the defensive team wins the ball, the offensive team that lost possession has to run through the gate and around the playing field (or a portion of it). All four defenders switch back to offense and take the place of the team that lost possession of the ball. Note that the defenders have to win possession of the ball—they can't just kick it out of the grid.
3. When the four offensive players return to the grid, they become the new defenders (two defenders in each grid).

Key Points

Players make short, support passes with an eye for the long pass out of the grid. The incentive for the offensive team is to get the ball out of the grid. The longer the ball stays in the grid, the more chances the defense will have to win possession.

One of the hardest aspects of this game is receiving the first pass from the opposite grid. The receiving player will have to quickly assess the position of the defenders and the teammates. Often a one-touch pass is the best play, especially if pressured tightly by a defender.

In some cases, the coach must act as arbitrator to determine which team is at fault for losing the ball. If there is any argument, have all players run around the field.

Variations

1. Vary the field size.
2. Designate a neutral zone between the two halves of the grid. Have two defenders start in the neutral zone until the ball enters the grid. (Two defenders challenge for the ball, the other two stay in the neutral zone and try to intercept the pass.)

Possession or Punishment

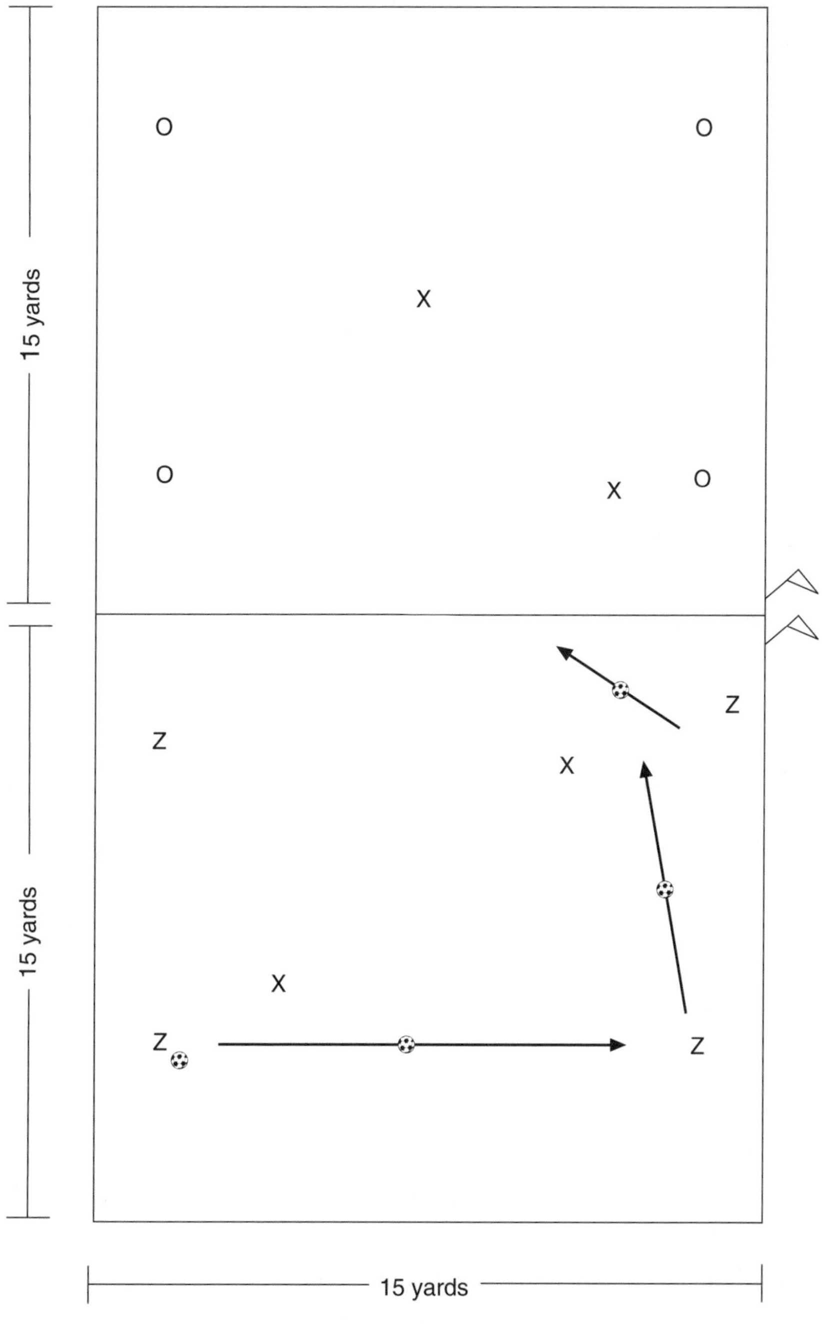

25 Link Pass

Purpose

To develop the ability to turn and pass to an unmarked teammate

Organization

Use 4 offensive players (per turn), 2 defenders. Player O_1 starts with the ball at midfield; 2 other players (O_3 and O_4) start near the top of the penalty area. Player 0_2 starts midway between other offensive players. Have 1 defender on top of the penalty area, 1 defender on the goal line next to the goalkeeper.

Procedure

1. Player O_1 starts play by passing to player O_2.
2. O_2 gathers the ball and continues play. As the ball is passed, O_2 should evaluate the position of the defenders.
3. Defender X_1 can either challenge the pass or mark either of the attackers. The second defender, X_2, can enter play if or when O_2 passes the ball.
4. The offensive players try to score on goal.
5. Restart with a new group of offensive players. Switch the defenders after several attempts.

Key Points

The ability of a midfield player to link a pass to an open forward can result in many scoring chances. The skilled midfielder, O_2 in this drill, has to assess his or her options before receiving the pass. Again, this is a skill that develops with practice. O_2's teammates (O_1, O_3, and O_4) can help by communicating the position of the defender. If O_2 passes back to O_1 (as in the variation), O_1 should continue play with an immediate pass forward to O_3 or O_4.

Variations

1. Enforce the offside rule.
2. Start with a chip instead of pass on the ground.
3. Add another defender who follows the ball into play from the first pass.
4. Allow a pass back to O_1, who can then pass forward to any open player.
5. Spread out the starting distance between O_3 and O_4.

Link Pass

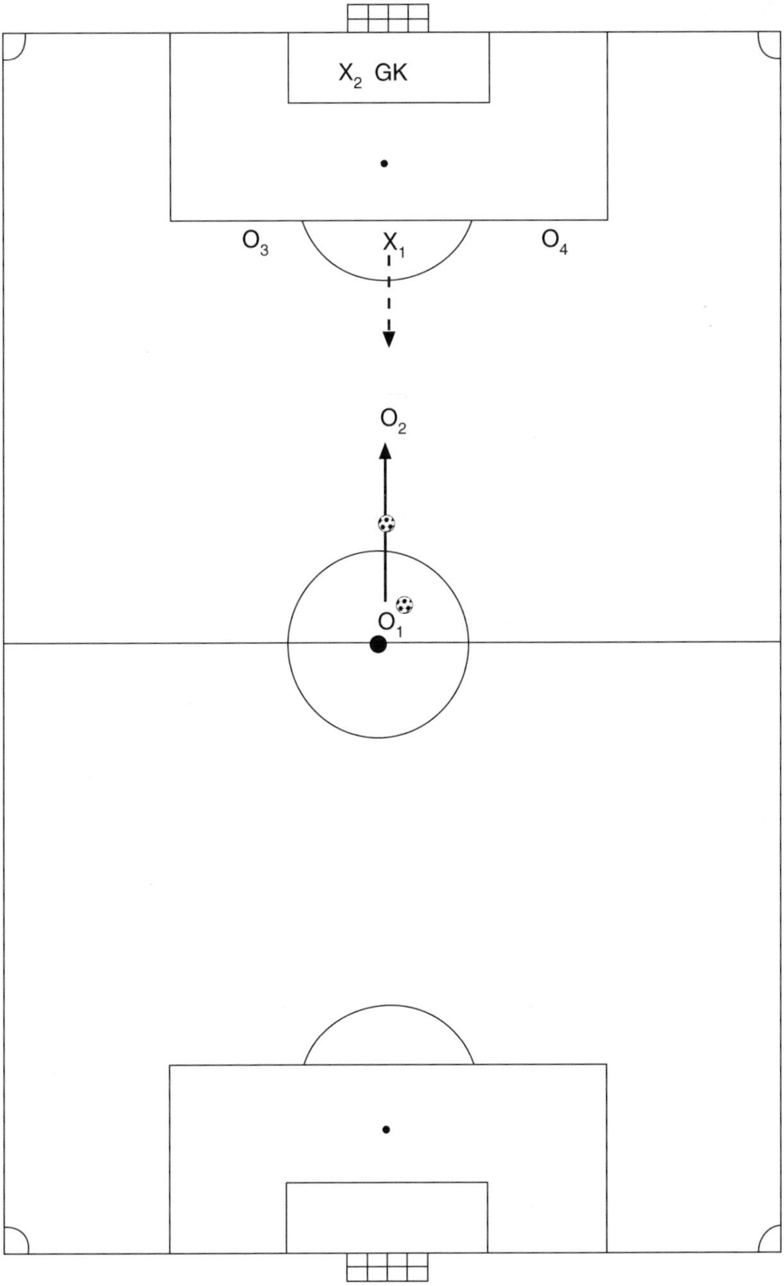

26 Second Pass

Purpose

To practice making checking runs, well-timed passes, and runs off the ball

Organization

Circle 10 to 15 yards in diameter; 4 players per circle, 2 vs. 1 inside the circle, 1 additional attacker outside the circle with the ball.

Procedure

1. The player with the ball passes to an open player.
2. The receiving player has one touch to play the ball to the other player in the grid. The sequence is complete if the ball can be played back to the outside player.
3. The outside player can move freely outside the circle.

Key Points

The first pass is easy; the second pass is extremely difficult, especially with a one-touch restriction. The first pass cannot be made until the second pass is possible, which is determined by the position of the second player relative to the defender. The player with the ball outside the grid evaluates and anticipates this positioning and makes the pass to the first player accordingly.

Patience is a virtue in this game. Don't rush the pass when the combination isn't on. Wait until the defender is drawn away and two passes are possible.

Variations

1. See which three players complete the sequence most often in one minute.
2. Play on top of the penalty area toward goal (instead of passing back outside the grid). Try putting the starting player to the side of the penalty area.
3. Start play with a throw-in from the perimeter of the circle.

Second Pass

26

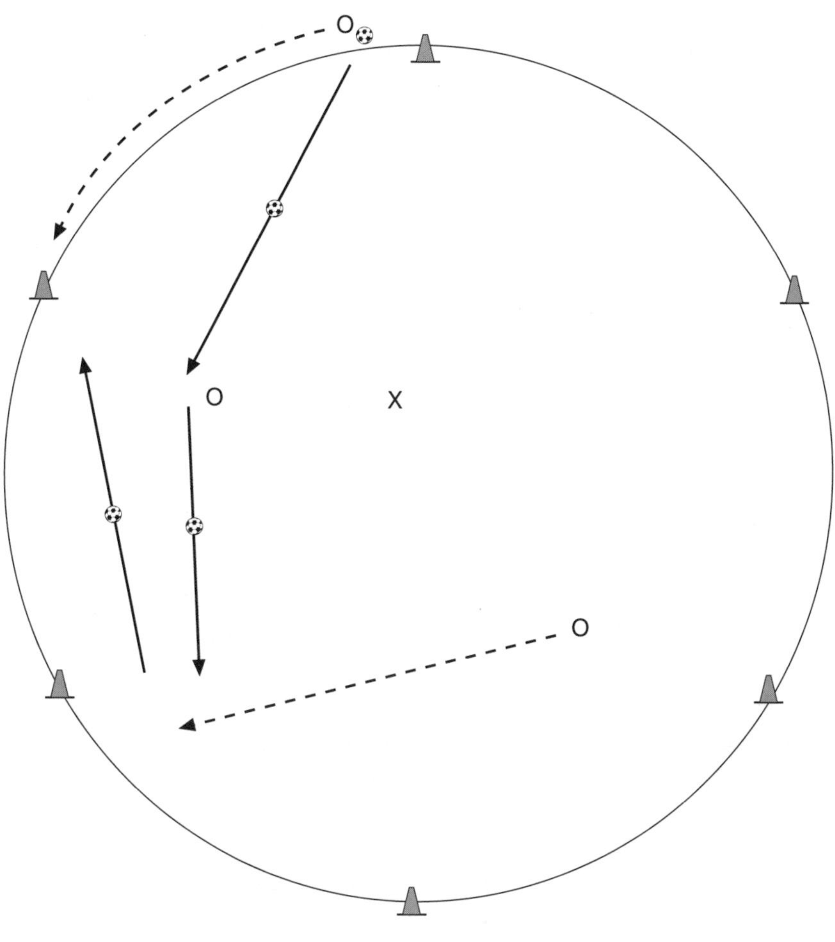

27 Throw-Ins

Purpose

To practice maintaining possession after a throw-in, moving off the ball

Organization

Create an alley with markers 10 to 15 yards parallel with the sideline. Use 7 players (4 attackers, 3 defenders) per turn; 1 offensive player with a ball on the sideline, 2 vs. 2 in the alley, and 1 vs. 1 in the middle of the field.

Procedure

1. Play starts with a throw-in from the offensive team.
2. After the throw-in, each team tries to maintain or to gain possession of the ball.
3. The middle players move up and down the field as targets.
4. A point is scored if a team can pass (or cross) the ball to their teammate in the middle of the field.
5. The thrower should enter play after the throw (creating a 3 vs. 2 in the alley).
6. If the ball goes out-of-bounds, restart play with a throw-in.

Key Points

The timing of the throw is as important as the accuracy. Players should experiment with checking runs, creating space both for themselves and for their teammates. They must give thought to what the player receiving the throw-in is going to do with the ball. The player must have an option before the ball is thrown. Players should also think about where to throw the ball. A throw to the feet is easier to control than one to the body. A throw to the head can be one touched back to the thrower or another teammate.

The throw-in is one of the few times in a game when a player has the luxury of time to make a decision. The longer the time, however, the longer the defense has to reorganize. In games it is often wise to throw the ball quickly. In this exercise, however, the throw is made when two teammates are best able to maintain possession against the two defenders.

Variations

1. Alter the position of the first throw-in.
2. Add another defender.

3. Allow the middle player to switch positions with a teammate in the grid. If one player leaves, he or she can enter.
4. Require the first player who touches the ball after the throw-in to pass it away in one touch.

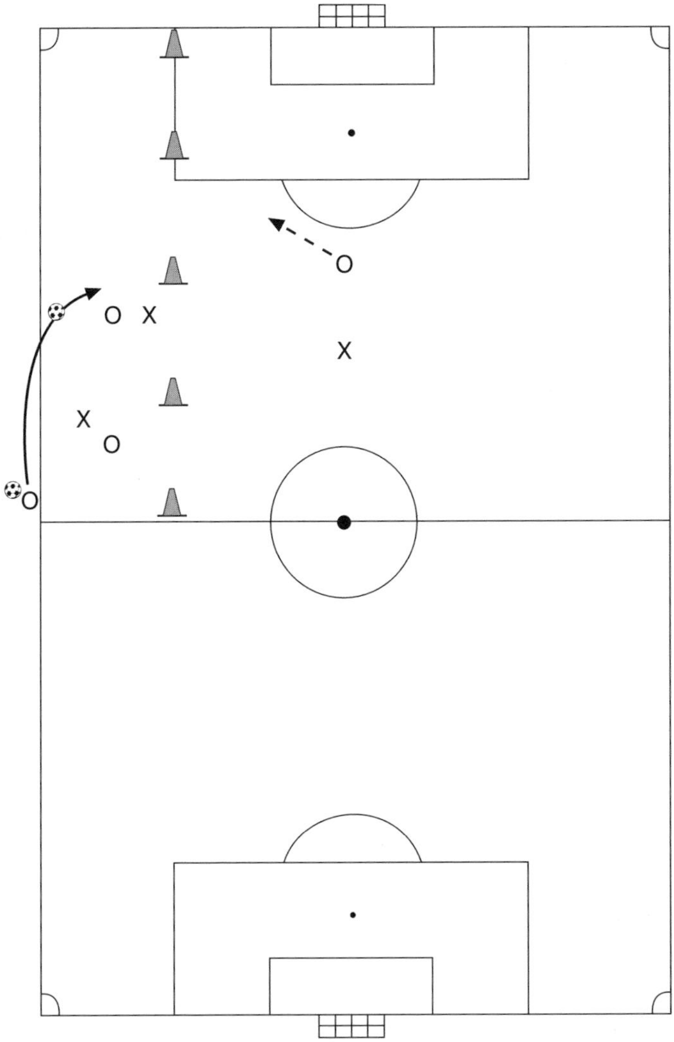

28 3 vs. 1 Squared

Purpose

To practice passing, shielding, assessing options

Organization

Make 2 grids, each 8 to 10 yards square, 15 to 20 yards apart. Use 8 players (3 vs. 1 in each grid), 1 ball per grid.

Procedure

1. Players play 3 vs. 1 keep-away in each grid.
2. On command one player leaves the first grid (*b*) and enters the second (*a*). When a player in the second grid passes to the player who enters from the first grid, the passer runs to the first grid, and so on.
3. Rotate defenders after several minutes of play, or if the defender can win the ball (not kick it out of the grid), he or she switches with the offensive player who lost the ball.

Key Points

In each grid three attackers play keep-away from one defender. When one attacker leaves the grid, however, a 2 vs. 1 results. The remaining players have to decide whether to hold the ball or pass. All the while the players are assessing the position of the supporting third player. The sooner this player arrives in the grid, the easier it will be to keep the ball away from the defender.

A longer distance between grids will increase the physical demand of the drill.

Variations

1. Alter the run of players when advancing from one grid to another. Lengthen the run by having players arch around a cone before entering the grid.
2. Have the entering player receive a pass outside the grid (then dribble into grid and continue passing).
3. Play 4 vs. 2 in any or all grids.
4. Play with three grids.

3 vs. 1 Squared

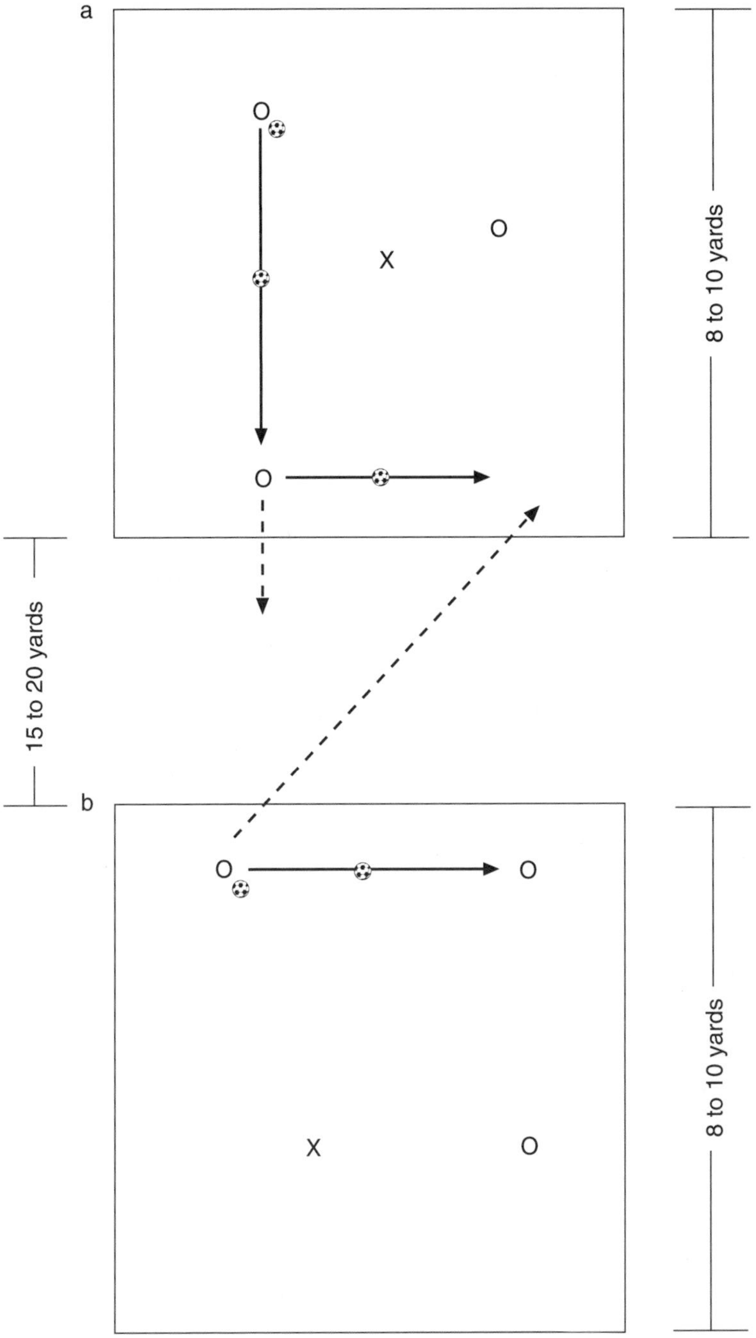

29 Restricted Touch Scrimmage

Purpose

To practice moving quickly into positions of support

Organization

Divide 8 to 22 players into 2 teams. Field size depends on the number of players.

Procedure

1. Play a regular scrimmage except each player is allowed a maximum of two touches per contact with the ball.
2. If the ball is touched more than twice, award the other team an indirect kick.

Key Points

Restricting touches is one of the classical methods to force players to *see the field.* Players need to anticipate what to do. It requires players without the ball to move into open passing lanes and communicate where they are before the player with the ball gets into trouble. Restricting the number of touches also forces players to *face the way they are playing.* That is, before the ball is received a player must position his or her body to properly see and execute the available options.

With only one or two touches the ball needs to be easily controlled. Likewise, players should consider what side of the body to pass the ball to.

When you award free kicks, encourage the nearest player to the ball to quickly restart the play.

Variations

To make the drill harder, do the following:

1. Allow only one touch per player.
2. Award a point for five consecutive passes or when every player on a team has touched the ball at least once.
3. The ball must be passed on the ground (or below the knees) or the other team is awarded possession.

To make the drill easier, do the following:

1. Allow three touches per player.
2. Allow dribbling (more than two touches) when the ball is in the penalty area.

Restricted Touch Scrimmage

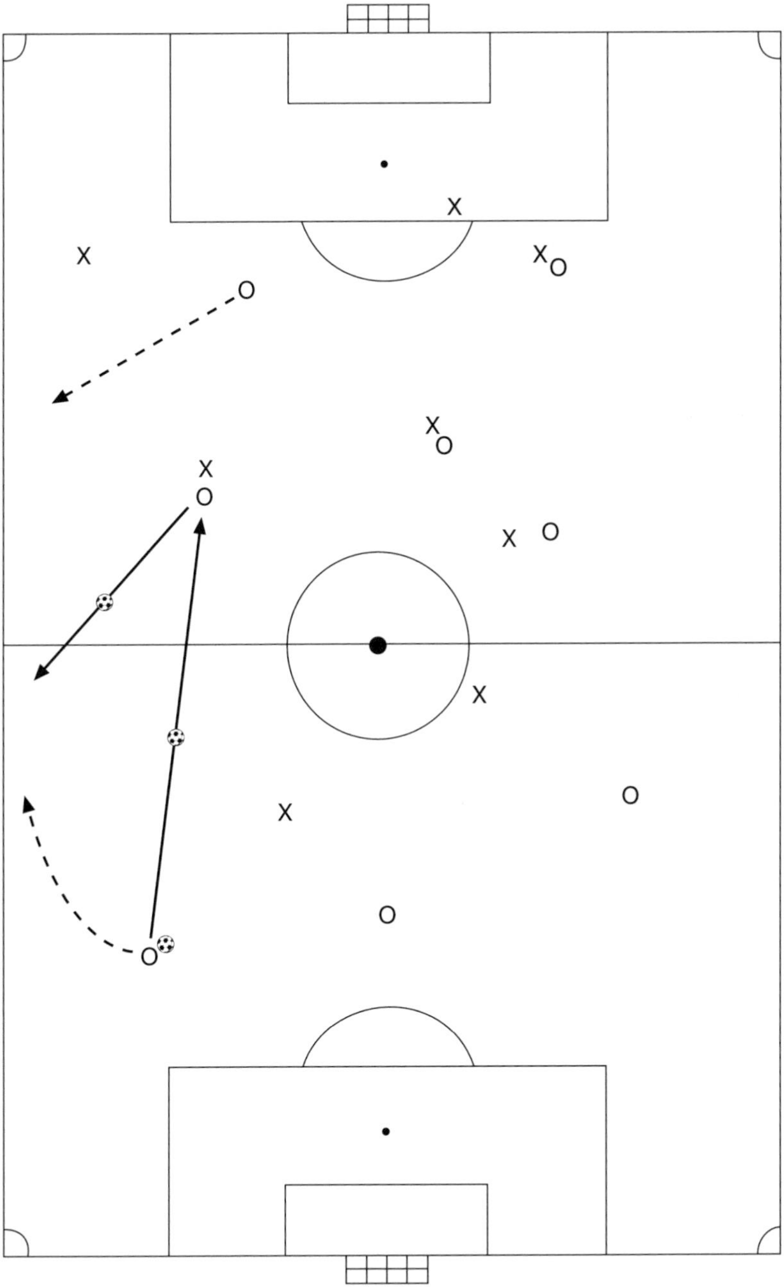

30 3 vs. 2 (With Point Players)

Purpose

To practice three-player passing combinations

Organization

Use 6 to 10 players. Position 2 attacking players near the top of the penalty area, each marked by a defender; 1 line of attacking players at the midfield line. The player at the front of the line starts with a ball; a keeper is in the goal.

Procedure

1. The player at the front of the line starts with the ball and tries to advance it by dribbling or passing to teammates.
2. Rotate new players in after each turn.

Key Points

This exercise requires good passing and well-timed runs. Have players experiment with passing combinations. The player with the ball can dribble straight to goal if not picked up by a defender. When a defender shifts toward the ball, the player dribbling should think pass. In this drill, one player should be open at all times. This player will have to read the defense and seize the opportunity. The attack toward goal should happen quickly. Players shouldn't need more than three passes before a shot on goal.

Variations

1. Start the three attackers in a line at midfield.
2. Remove one defender.
3. Add a third defender (sweeper) who starts behind the other defenders.

3 vs. 2 (With Point Players)

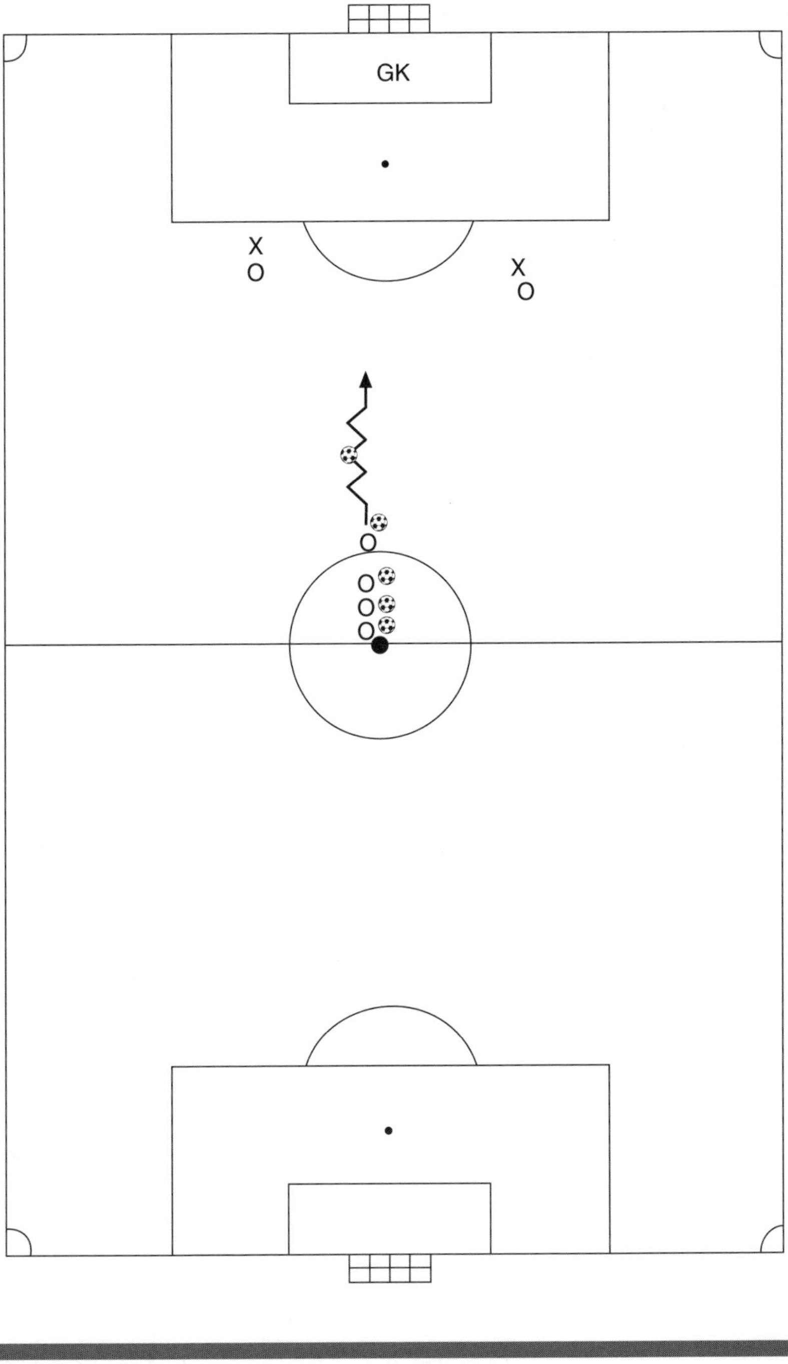

31 Tight Marking

Purpose

To practice shooting under pressure, showing for the ball

Organization

Grid 20 by 20 yards with a goal on each end, divided into 4 squares; 10 players (2 teams of 5 players each) plus 2 goalkeepers. Each square of the grid has a 1 vs. 1. The fifth players can roam freely within the grid.

Procedure

1. Each team defends one goal and tries to score on the other. Four players from each team have to stay in their respective squares. The fifth can roam freely.
2. Play starts with the goalkeeper rolling the ball out to a player.
3. Players can shoot or pass at any time.
4. Play continues until either team scores or the ball goes out-of-bounds.

Key Points

In this shooting exercise, players practice passing, dribbling, and shooting with tight defensive pressure. Quick runs, sharp passes, and good dribbling will result in shots on goal.

To receive a pass the offensive player will have to create space by leading the defender away, then checking back to the ball. An angled approach to the ball makes it easier to turn after receiving the ball.

The defenders should be marking goalside. The defender tries to deny the turn. The body will be used to shield the ball. When the ball is won, an immediate counterattack to goal should occur.

Variations

1. Set up a larger field with 2 vs. 2 in each square.
2. Allow players to leave the square, but they can only touch the ball once (one touch) then they must return to their square.
3. Remove the fifth player from each team.

Tight Marking

31

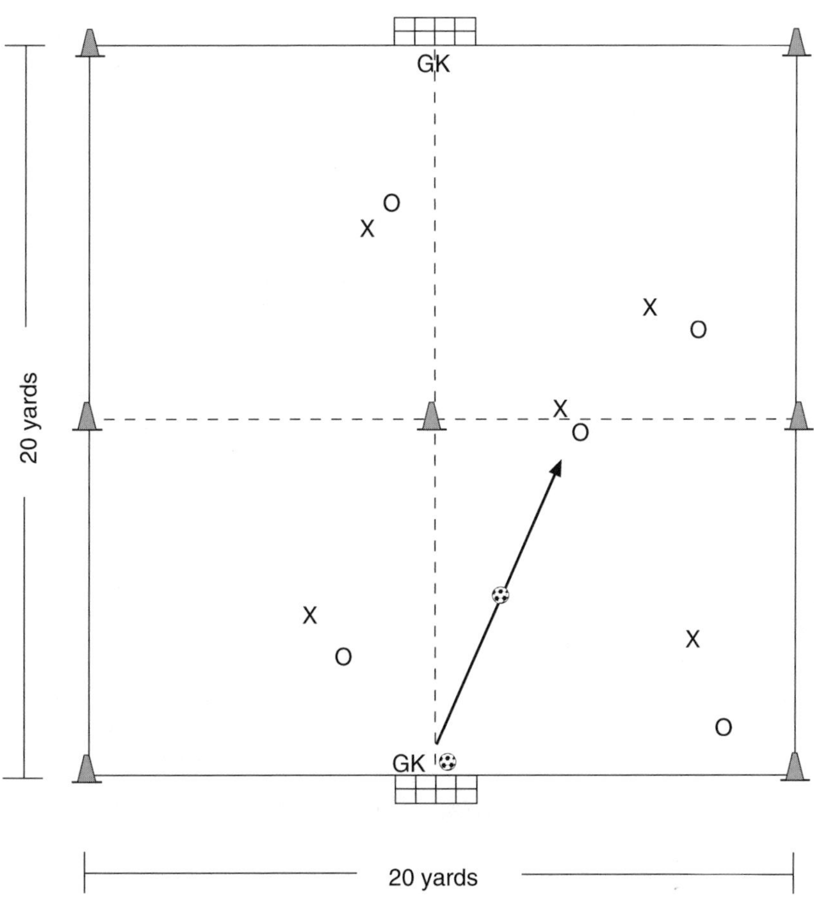

Courtesy of Indiana University/Guy Zimmer

CHAPTER 3

Applying Advanced Skills

Skillful soccer players perform fundamental skills successfully and consistently. Occasionally players will make plays or perform acts that require an advanced skill. These advanced skills are the focus of the drills in this chapter.

Advanced skills are remarkable by their infrequency of use. They include such acts as the heel pass, the swerving kick, the side volley, and the diving header—skills not commonly identified as fundamental.

Emphasize that players should minimize advanced technique or flashy play in favor of simple and sound play. The advanced skills are tools to use when the fundamentals fail. In these situations, advanced skills will broaden the scope of options available to players.

Because the situations occur rarely, players will have little opportunity to improve these skills just playing or scrimmaging. This chapter isolates these skills in a practice setting and asks players to perform the skills repetitively. When possible, the skills are set into the context of a game situation.

By practicing these advanced techniques, players will have the comfort and confidence to know whether they can accomplish the act—or try it at all—in the game. Advanced players, like all serious athletes, should know their weaknesses as well as their strengths.

32 Ball Control on the Run

Purpose

To practice dribbling, passing, and receiving while running

Organization

Form 4 lines with 8 to 20 players, 2 in the corners on the same end of the field, 1 on each side of the midfield line.

Procedure

1. The player at the front of the line in one corner of the field starts by dribbling the ball at full speed toward the first player in line on the opposite side of the field at the midfield line. This player can pass to the second player at any time.
2. The pair tries to advance the ball to the opposite end line as quickly as possible.
3. The pair is done when the ball is stopped on the end line and both players cross over the end line.
4. Reset from the other direction and continue.

Key Points

This drill requires players to dribble on the run, pass on the run, and receive the ball on the run. When dribbling, the player should contact the ball while maintaining a natural running stride. To do this the player contacts the ball with the top of the feet, toe pointed down, near the end of the stride.

The pass from the first player should be to the space ahead of the running second player. Evaluate if the second player can run onto the pass without breaking stride. Of equal importance is how the receiving player gathers the pass. Are the players able to control the ball on the run? Does the first touch direct the ball ahead into space? Is the ball in play with minimal bounce in front of the running player?

Variations

1. Two groups proceed at the same time (one ball at each corner) and race to the end line.
2. Add a defender who starts near midfield or at the far end line. Let one pair at a time take a turn.
3. Change the starting position of the second player (e.g., the opposite end line). Changing this position will affect when the first player passes the ball and how the second player receives it.
4. Shorten the length of the playing area.

Ball Control on the Run

32

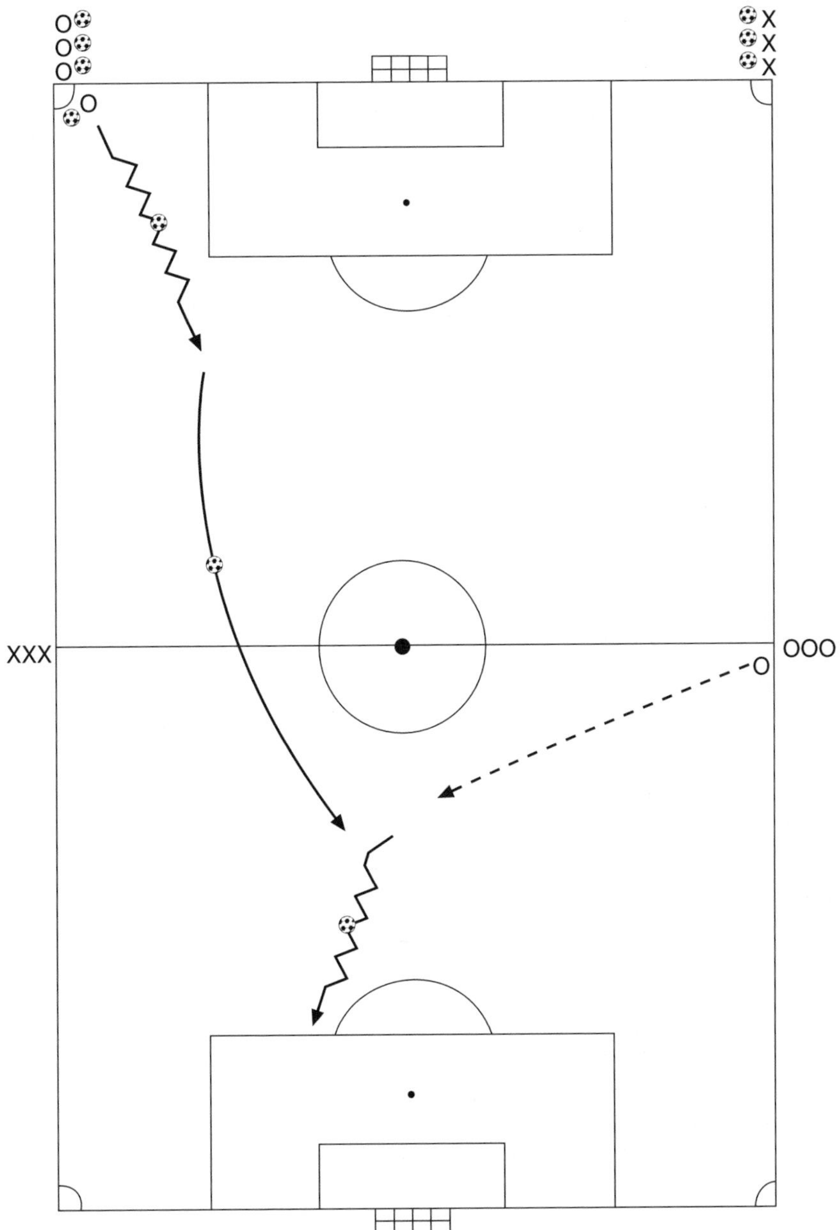

33 Counterclockwise I (Half Field)

Purpose

To practice receiving, passing, and shooting

Organization

Form 2 lines of 8 to 16 players, 1 between corner of penalty area and sideline, the other near the midfield line. The goalkeeper is in the goal area with a supply of balls.

Procedure

1. Goalkeeper starts play by throwing the ball ahead of the first person in the line to the right of the penalty area. This player controls the ball, then passes it into the center.
2. The first player from the other line gathers the ball and shoots before entering the penalty area.
3. Players switch lines after each turn.

Key Points

This is an excellent pregame warm-up (after stretching). Players move continuously while practicing a variety of skills. The goalkeeper should throw the ball ahead of the running player. Have the player stay wide then run diagonally toward the center to meet the ball. Try to have players pull the ball back toward the goal. They should dribble for a few touches toward the midfield line then pass the ball back toward the top of the penalty area. While dribbling, players glance over the left shoulder and identify the position of the forward. On the kick the plant foot is placed next to the ball then pivoted so the toe points in the intended direction of the pass.

Variations

1. Start a defender on the end line. The defender enters play the moment the pass to the center is made.
2. Change the position of the lines and run the exercise in the opposite direction (clockwise).
3. Require a chip pass into the center.

Counterclockwise I (Half Field)

GK

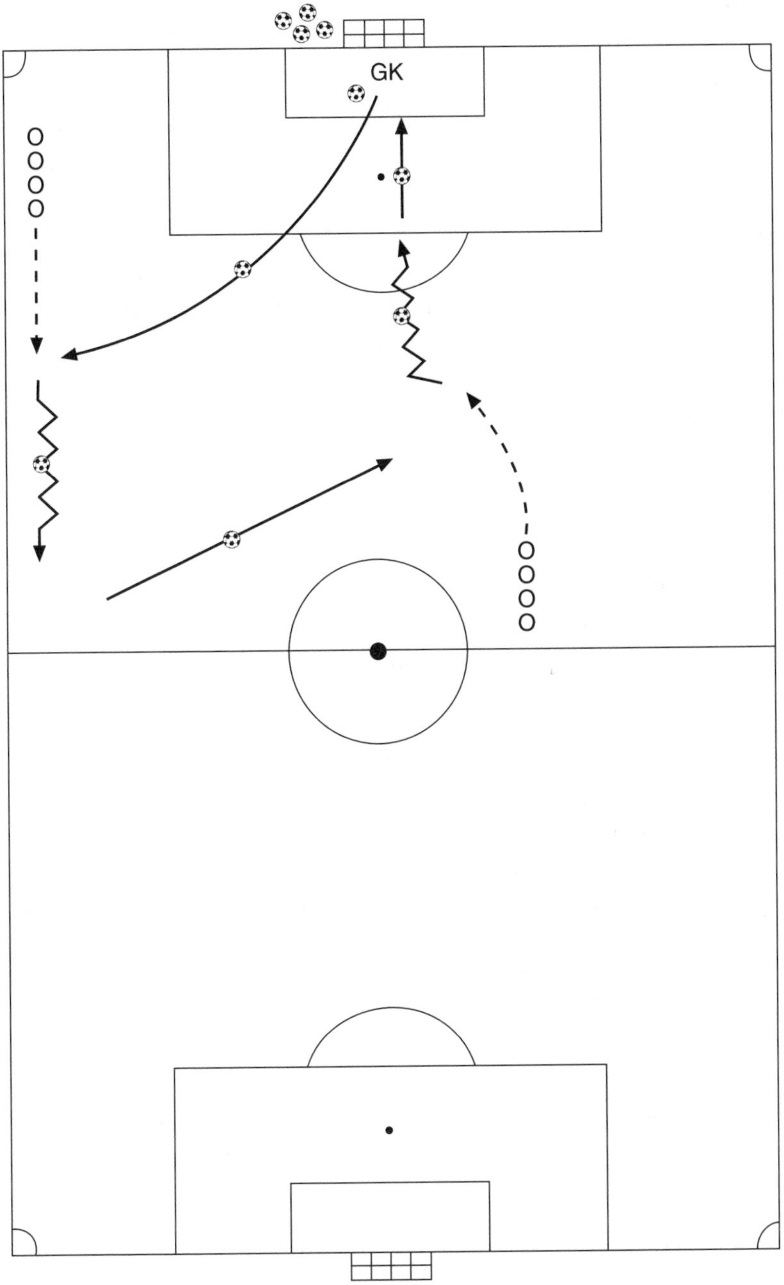

34 Counterclockwise II (Full Field)

Purpose

To practice through passing, shooting, receiving

Organization

With 16 to 20 players, form 4 lines of 4 to 5 players each, 1 line to the right of each penalty area, 2 lines at midfield. Goalkeepers are in each goal with a supply of balls.

Procedure

1. The goalkeeper starts play by throwing a ball to the player at the front of the line to the right of the penalty area. This player gathers the ball and passes it forward to the player running from the front of the line near midfield.
2. The receiver gathers the ball on the run and shoots on goal before entering the penalty area.
3. The goalkeeper at the opposite end of the field continues play in the other direction. Try for two balls in play at one time.

Key Points

The passes should be led into the space ahead of the running players. Players gathering the pass should do so while maintaining forward momentum. Players should not have to break stride to gather the ball. When running with the ball (with no immediate defensive pressure), players should touch the ball every third or fourth step. The first touch should settle the bounce and direct the ball in the direction of the run.

The shooting players should continue at goal for several touches. They should shoot while moving forward. Have players glance up before shooting to assess the position of the goalie. When the passive defender is in place (in the variation), a player should dribble by with a sharp change of pace, then shoot on the first or second touch after passing the defender.

Variations

1. Add a passive defender in each half of the field. Defender starts on top of the penalty area.
2. End play with a cross. Have several forwards and several defenders play in the penalty area (2 vs. 1, 2 vs. 2, or more).
3. Play in the opposite direction (clockwise).

Counterclockwise II (Full Field)

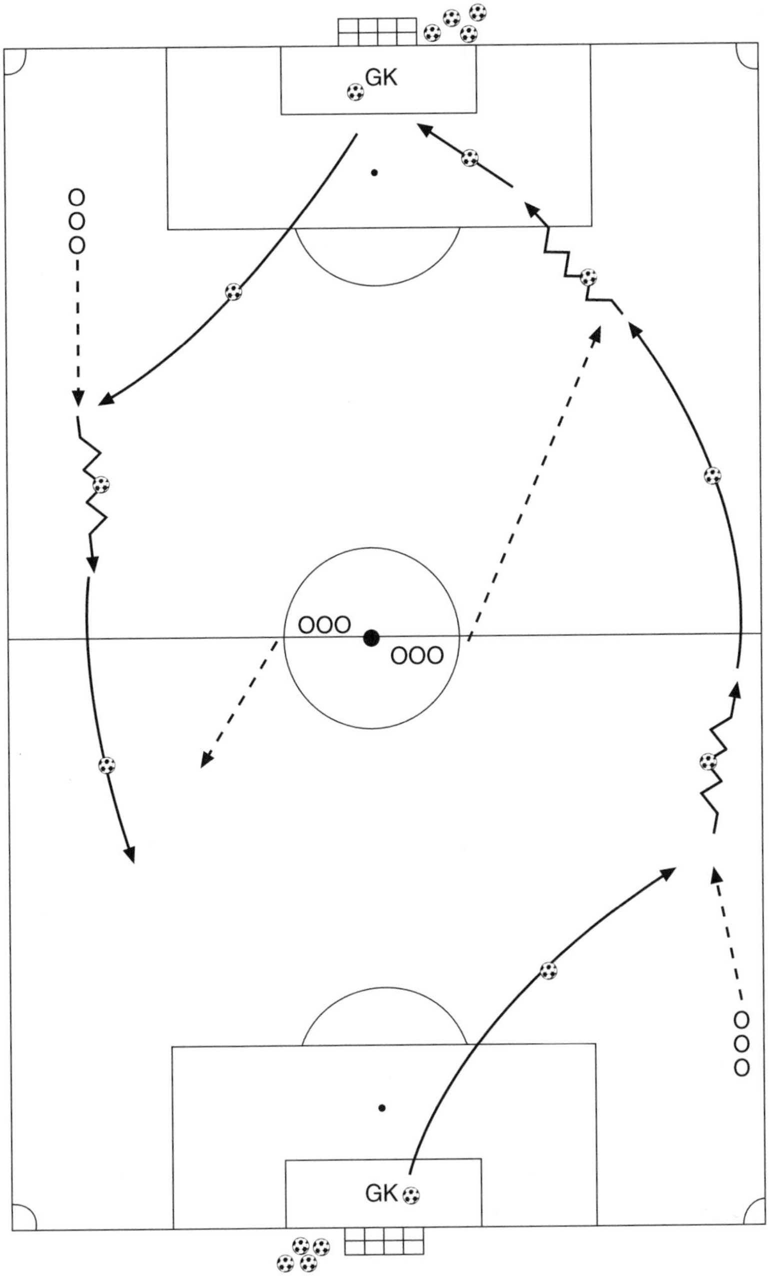

35 Nondominant Leg

Purpose

To develop the ability to kick and control the ball with the nondominant leg.

Organization

Players pair up and face each other, 10 yards apart, 1 ball per pair.

Procedure

Players pass back and forth, progressing through the following passing sequence using only the weaker or less dominant leg.

1. One touch, 10 yards apart, inside of the passing foot.
2. Two touch, 10 yards apart, inside of foot on first touch, inside of foot on second touch.
3. Two touch, 10 yards apart, outside first touch, inside second touch.
4. Two touch, 10 yards apart, first touch either foot, second touch instep of nondominant foot.
5. Low drive, 20 yards apart, stationary ball.
6. Low drive, 25 yards apart, ball rolling forward on kick (first touch controls ball and rolls it forward).

Key Points

For many players the only way to develop the accuracy and power of the nondominant leg is with forced repetitions. Only through practice will a player develop comfort and control. By being able to play with both feet, the player has more options.

In the two-touch drills the first touch controls the ball and sets it up for the second touch or pass. In the one-touch exercises, consider the pace or *weight* of the pass. Can the partner realistically one touch it back? Both players should be up on their toes ready to move into the path of the ball.

The nonkicking leg is as important as the kicking leg. Players need to balance, then swing through the ball. Watch the follow-through of the kicking leg. A poor follow-through will highlight problems with the kicking motion. Is the nonkicking foot placed next to the ball? Is the toe of the plant foot pointed at the target? Is the player watching the ball on contact?

Variation

Have players work in groups of three.

Nondominant Leg

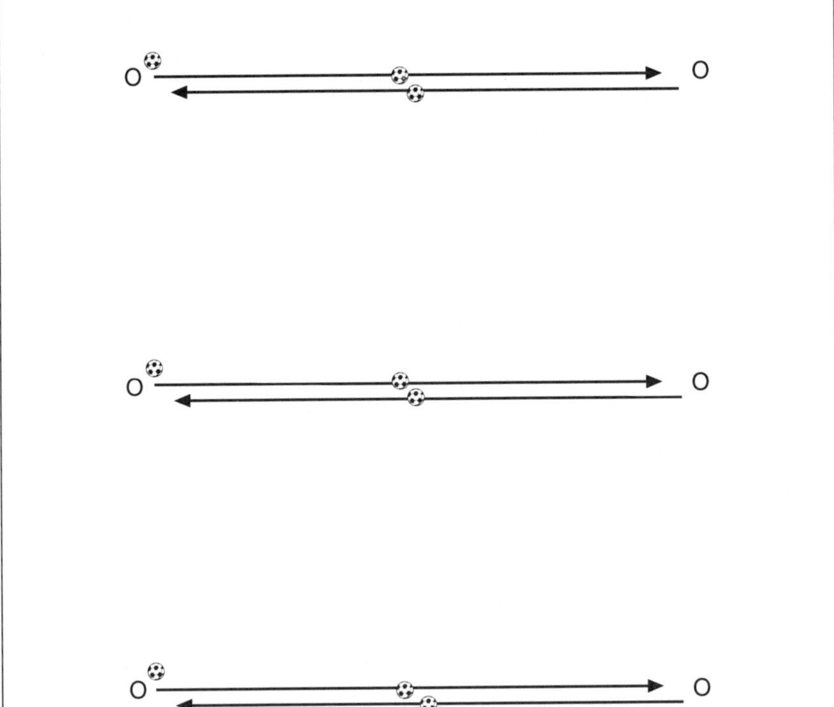

36 Chip Pass

Purpose

To work on chipping, shooting, and controlling the ball on the run

Organization

Form 2 lines at midfield, 5 or 6 players per line with a goalkeeper in the goal. The player at the head of 1 line has the ball.

Procedure

1. The player at the head of one line runs into the space 15 yards ahead of the line. The player with the ball at the front of the other line chips the ball over the head of the first player.
2. The player gathers the ball then shoots on goal. The ball must be shot before the top of the penalty area.

Key Points

The chip pass can send the ball over numerous defenders. To keep the ball from *running* the player should apply a backspin. This spin will deaden the bounce and make the ball easier to control on the receiving end. The player applies the spin with a short, choppy kick, contacting the ball near the ground with the top of the foot near the toes. The toes flick slightly upward as they make contact under the ball. The chip has virtually no follow-though.

Variations

1. Have the running player enter play from a different angle.
2. Require the first player to dribble then chip the ball. Start the first line behind the midfield line.
3. Add a defender who starts on the goal line.
4. Start the lines near the sidelines. Have the first player receive the ball then cross it into the center to the second player.

Chip Pass

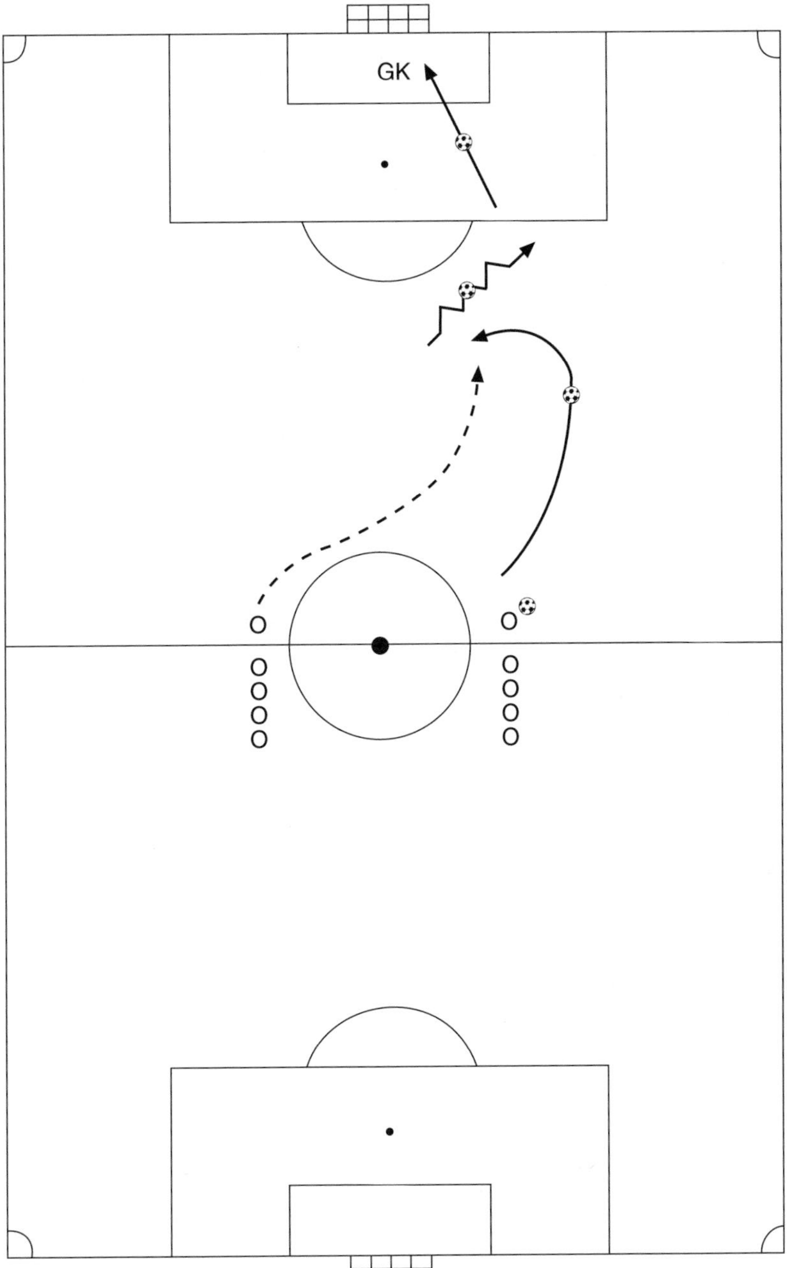

37 Heel Pass

Purpose

To practice advanced passing technique, changing the direction of play

Organization

Form 2 lines near midfield, with 8 to 16 players and a goalkeeper in the goal. Players in 1 of the lines start with balls.

Procedure

1. The player with the ball dribbles diagonally toward the corner of the penalty area.
2. The first player from the other line runs in toward the goal.
3. The dribbling player slows or stops near the top of the penalty area and heel passes the ball to the other player. This player gathers the ball and shoots on goal. The player who just heel passed continues running into the corner.

Key Points

The heel pass can be effective in certain situations. If a player is trapped by defenders or stuck in the corner, the heel pass may be the only chance of getting the ball to a supporting player.

The point of the heel contacts the ball near the midline. The plant foot is next to the ball. The pass is hard to perform on the run. The player should slow first, then execute it.

A fake heel pass can also be effective. The heel travels over the ball. This action can cause the defender to stop or transfer his or her weight.

Variations

1. Alter the angle of the dribble toward goal.
2. Add a defender who starts near the top of the penalty area. Allow the attacker the option to pass or to continue dribbling.

Heel Pass

GK

Heel pass

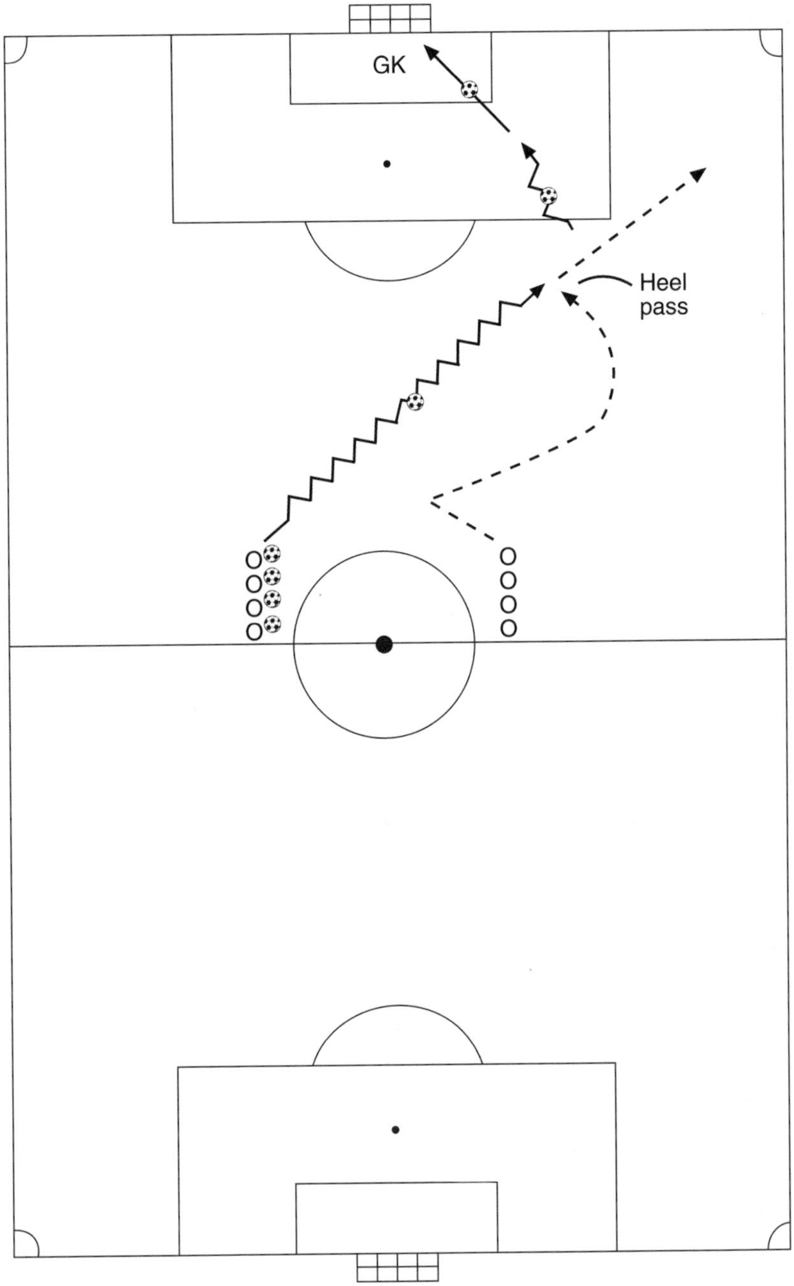

38 Flick Pass

Purpose

To practice deceptive passing on the run, overlap runs

Organization

Make 3 lines of attacking players (10 yards apart) on the end line, 3 passive defenders spaced evenly on the field, 1 ball for each group of 3 attackers.

Procedure

1. The first three players in each line form a group. Each group takes a turn advancing down the field, passing the ball back and forth. Players should work on passing the ball with the outside of the foot while running forward.
2. The ball starts with the middle player, O_2. O_2 passes to O_3, then overlaps O_3 to the outside. O_3 now becomes the middle player and passes to O_1. O_3 overlaps O_1 on the outside.
3. Defenders put slight pressure on the ball. When one group of three gets to the end line, have them wait for the rest of the groups to finish. Then the groups come back the other way.

Key Points

Watch that the passes are timed and paced well. Players shouldn't have to break stride or run backward to gather bad passes. The ball should be led into the space ahead of the running players. The flow of the drill is key. At best, players can do these drills on a sprint using one- or two-touch passes.

Players can use this drill to practice the flick pass. Perform the flick pass by passing with the front foot as it moves into the next step. The toes turn slightly inside, with the ankle firm. At the last moment the foot flicks to advance the ball into space. The player makes the pass while running in stride. The nonkicking foot is not placed alongside the ball.

The advantage of the pass is that it has an element of deception. The player can make it without breaking stride. The defender doesn't know if the ball will be dribbled or passed until the last moment of contact.

The flick pass is also used for layoffs, bending passes down the line, or for quick give-and-goes.

Variations

1. Straight line passing—players run in straight lines while passing the ball back and forth the distance of the field.
2. End each turn with a shot on goal.
3. Increase pressure from the defenders. Allow players to advance the ball by dribbling or passing as they see fit (no predetermined runs or patterns).

Flick Pass

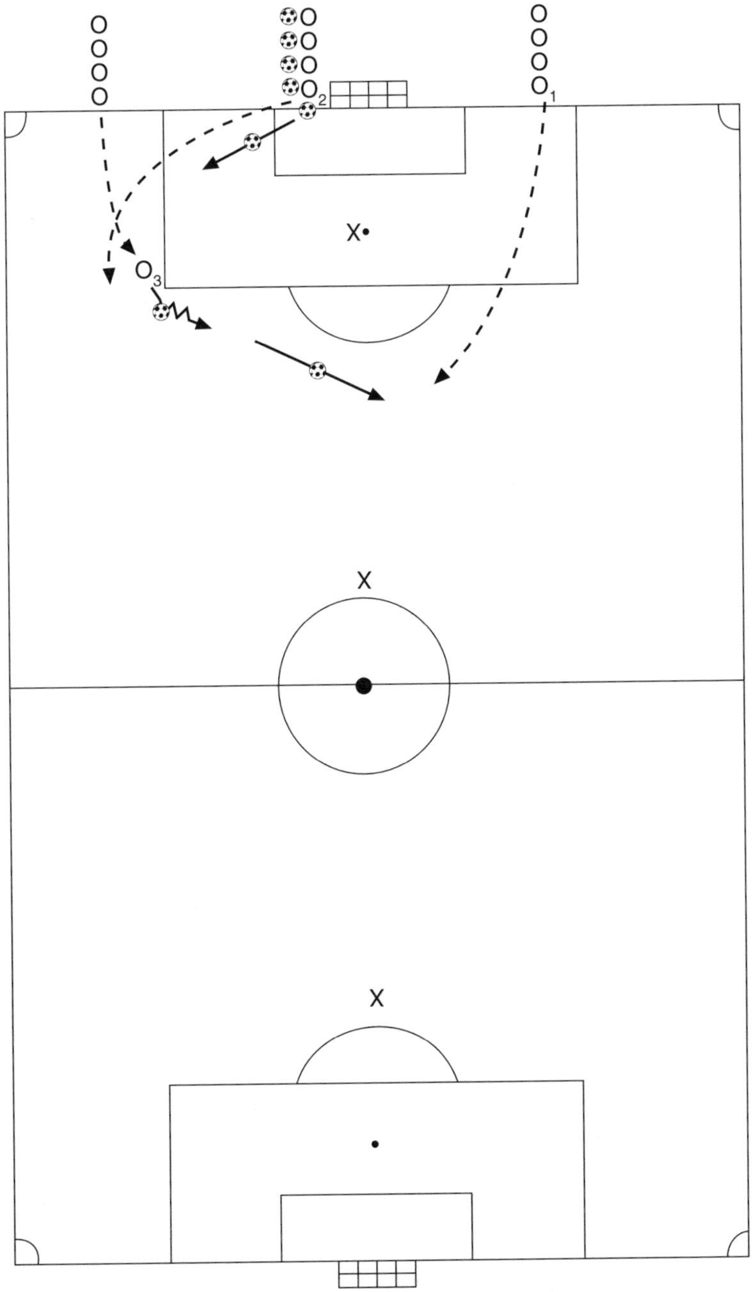

39 Long Drives

Purpose

To practice switching the ball from one side of the field to the other

Organization

Form 4 lines with 8 to 20 players, 2 lines on either side of the goal. All the balls start on the inside line on 1 side of the goal.

Procedure

1. The player with the ball passes it forward into the space ahead of the outside line.
2. The player at the head of the outside line receives the ball and drives it across the field.
3. Either player from the other side goes to meet the ball, controls it, then passes it to the outside for the other player to drive it back across the field. The player who does not receive the ball should make an overlap run to the outside of the player who does control it.
4. Once all groups have finished, return in the opposite direction.

Key Points

The long, low drive is difficult because only a small part of the foot contacts the ball. Slight adjustments will affect the height and distance of the kick. Rhythm, timing, and proper contact—as in a golf swing—are more important than sheer power. If players are having difficulties with this drill, have them practice this kick with stationary balls.

In games, the best pass is often the longest if possession can be maintained. The long pass switches the point of attack and forces the defense to restructure.

Variations

1. Play one touch.
2. Require the receiving player to pass the ball back (to the inside or outside) for the second player to play across the field.

Long Drives

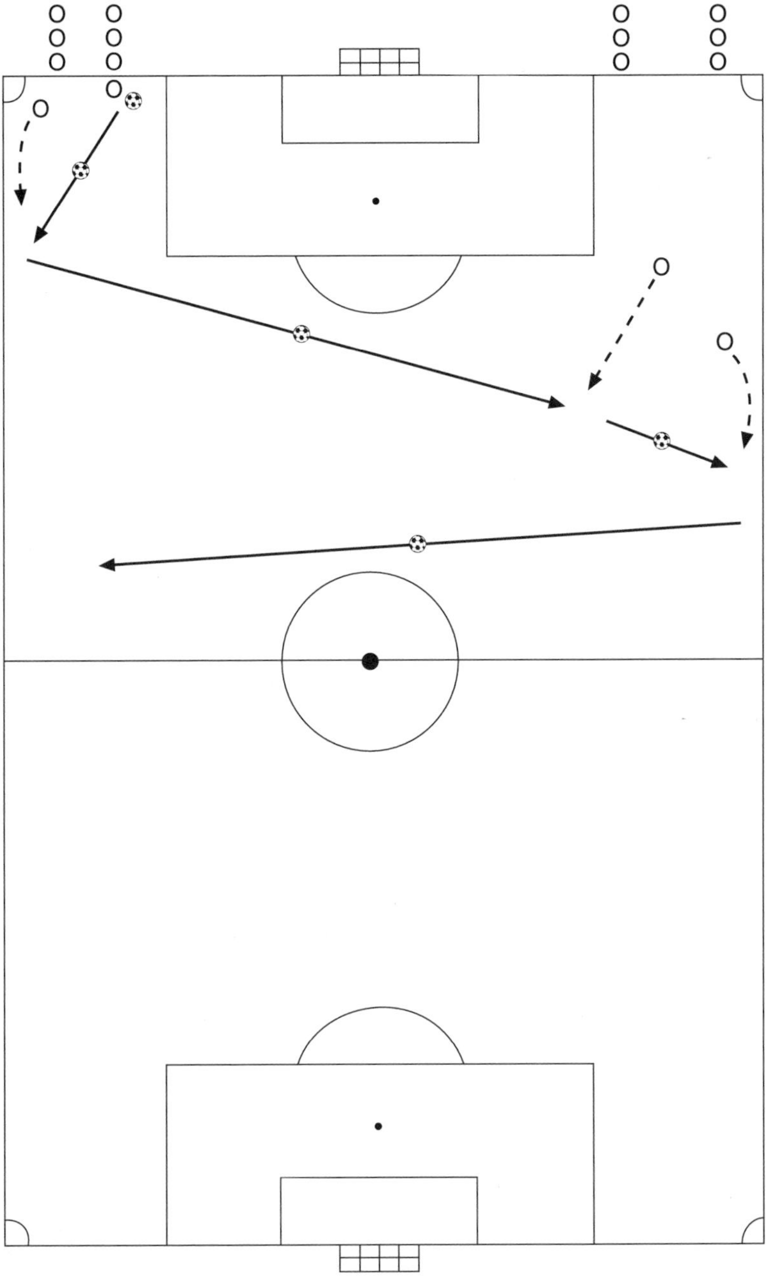

40 Power-Shot Progression

Purpose

To practice shooting with power and accuracy

Organization

Players form 2 lines 20 yards out from each goal post (no more than 4 players per line). Set up another goal and 2 more lines of shooters if need be. Goalkeepers are in goals.

Procedure

Players practice shooting in a variety of situations while focusing on the follow-through of the kick. Progress through the following:

1. The first player in line rolls the ball forward several feet and shoots on goal. After the kick, players should land on the kicking foot. (The body's momentum is carried through the kick, and the plant foot comes off the ground after the kick. The player lands on the kicking foot several feet in front of where he or she contacted the ball.) Players switch lines after each turn.
2. All balls start in one of the two lines. The player at the front of the line passes the ball diagonally in front of the first player in the other line. This player shoots on goal. The first player runs toward goal to play the rebound. Start balls in the other line after each player has several turns.

Key Points

Occasionally during a game a player will have the time and space to *wind up* for a sheer power shot. (In other shooting situations, the defensive pressure is so tight around the goal that the shooter is forced to take a quick shot while moving laterally, falling, or otherwise unbalanced.)

The power in this technique comes from solid contact with the ball and follow-through. Emphasize the follow-though in this progression and ask the player to land on the kicking foot. (As the player kicks the ball away, the heel of the plant foot raises off the ground and momentum lifts the player's entire foot off the ground and forward.)

All other rules of proper shooting still apply: head and knee over ball on contact, ankle stiff, toe pointed down. Have players watch the ball on contact. Repetition will result in fluidity of motion and increased player confidence.

Players should aim for the far post in most cases. A low, well struck ball to the far post is one of the most difficult shots for the goalkeeper to save.

Variation

1. Add a third line of defenders that starts between the two other lines. The defender follows the pass into play and applies pressure to the shooter.

Power-Shot Progression

40

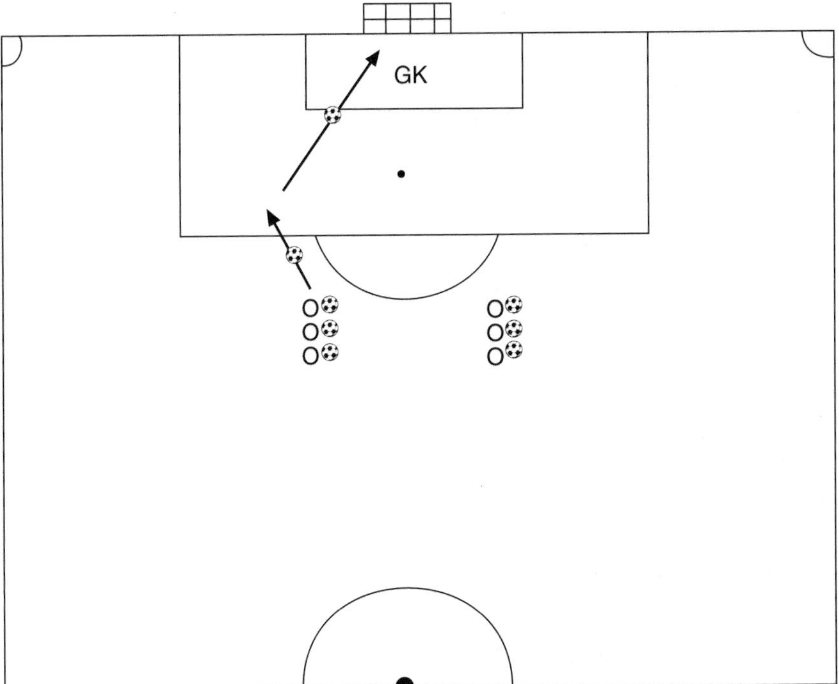

41 Quick Shot

Purpose

To practice shooting in tight pressure—quick, deceptive shooting

Organization

Line up 5 to 10 balls 1 yard apart inside the penalty area, 1 player at a time, a goalkeeper in the goal. (You can set up a duplicate organization with another goal if you have too many players for 1 setup.)

Procedure

1. Each player takes a turn shooting a series of balls in quick succession. Instruct players to shoot quickly. Shoot, step, shoot, step, and so on.
2. Because this exercise takes considerable time to set up for each player, rotate players out from another, ongoing activity or scrimmage. Have each player go at least twice, once from each direction.

Key Points

Most shooting opportunities come and go in a flash. Attackers gain considerable advantage if they can maximize these rare occurrences. The quick shot comes more from the knee than the hip. The player does not have time to flex the hip and may not be carrying any forward momentum. Players often perform this shot off a pivot or quick lateral movement. A toe kick can also be advantageous for performing a quick shot (especially if the player has to reach for the ball).

The quick shot is deceptive in that defenders and goalkeepers don't necessarily see the shot coming. (A shot with a big wind-up and hip flex is telegraphed.)

Variation

A server with a supply of balls (and a helper) quickly rolls or throws balls into the shooter. Vary the angle of the serve. The helper should hand balls to the server.

Quick Shot

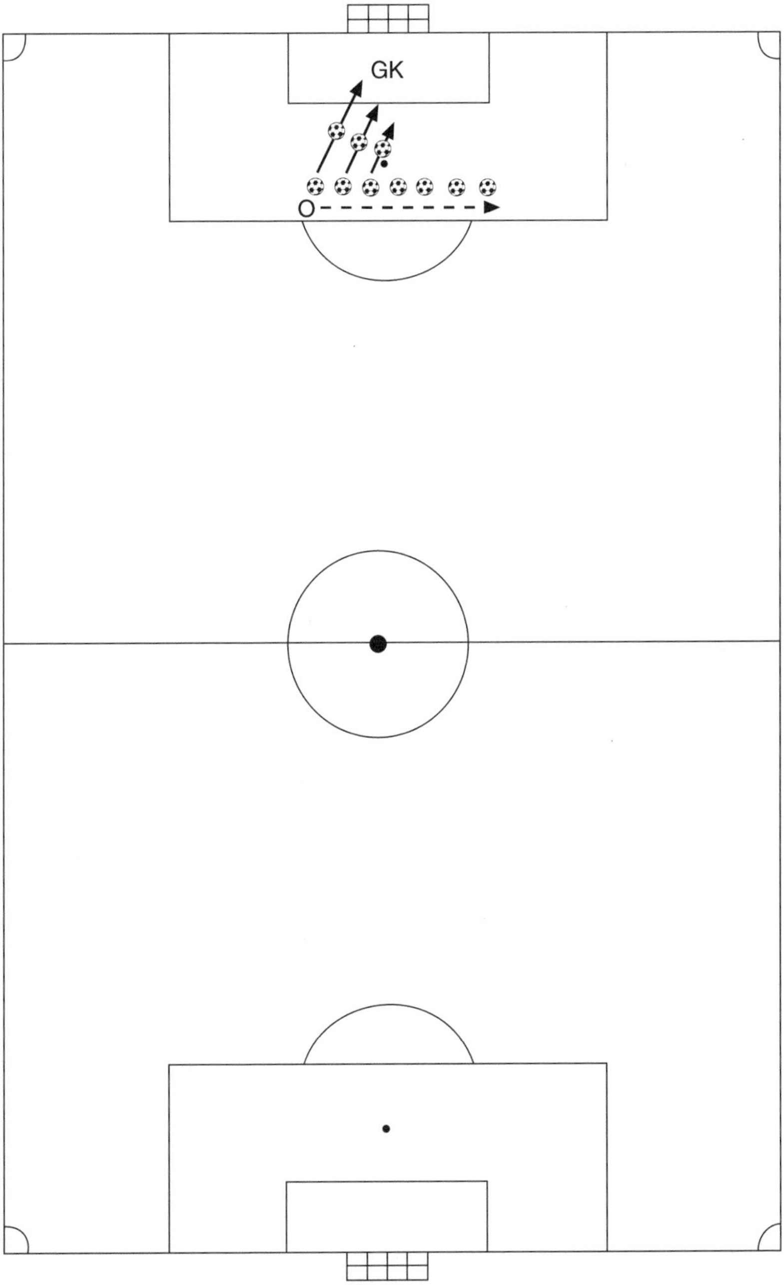

42 Scissors Kick

Purpose

To practice performing the overhead scissors (or bicycle) kick

Organization

Arrange players in pairs, 1 ball per pair.

Procedure

One player in each pair stands on the top of the penalty box with his or her back to the goal. The players take turns shooting on goal using the scissors kick, progressing through the following:

1. Players serve balls to themselves by tossing them overhead, then scissors kick. Each partner takes several attempts.
2. Partners face each other five yards apart as in *a*. The player farthest from the goal is facing the goal. This player throws the ball above the head of the partner with his or her back to the goal. (Underhand throw works best.) Players can also throw the ball to the side of the player whose back is to the goal.
3. Players form a line above the penalty area as in *b*. A server crosses in balls from the sideline. The player at the front of the line tries to scissors kick to goal.

Caution: The scissors kick is dangerous (even if done properly). It is a difficult skill that should be taught to older, advanced players. It should never be done in a congested area near other players.

Key Points

To perform the kick, the nonkicking leg comes off the ground first to help propel the body upward and backward. As the kicking foot goes to meet the ball, the nonkicking foot makes a quick move back toward the ball (like blades of scissors coming together). When the top of the foot contacts the ball, the nonkicking foot moves into a position alongside the ball. Players should try to drive the ball down. They must watch the ball when kicking it.

Players can perform this kick to the side of the body as well. The principle is the same for any powerful kick in which both feet leave the ground.

Instruct players to use the arms for balance and to help break the fall.

Variations

1. Players scissors kick balls thrown from the side of the penalty area.
2. Try any of the scissors kick activities on balls tossed to the side of the body (between hip and head height).

Scissors Kick

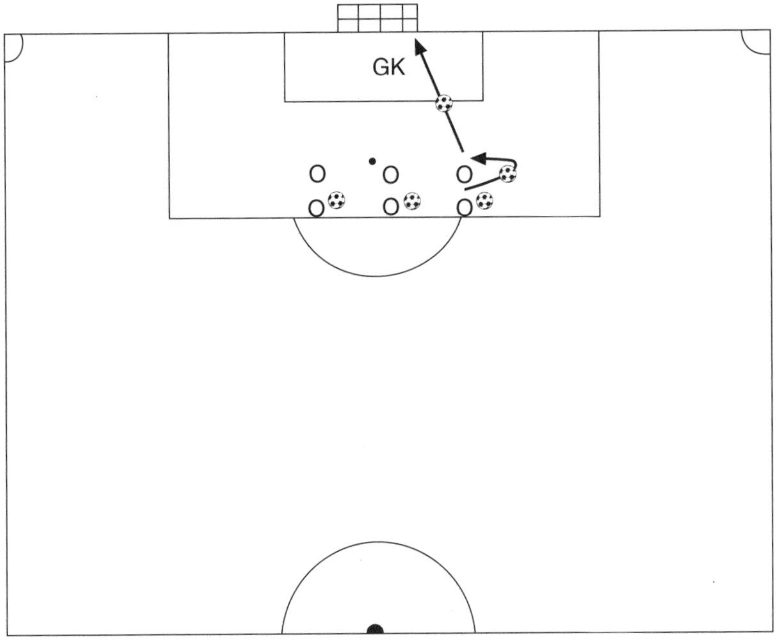

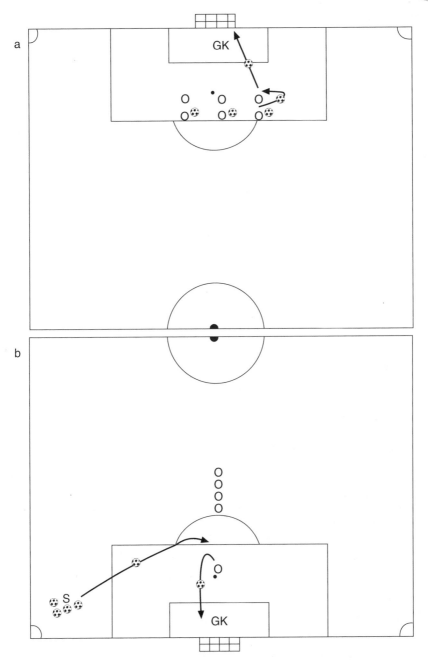

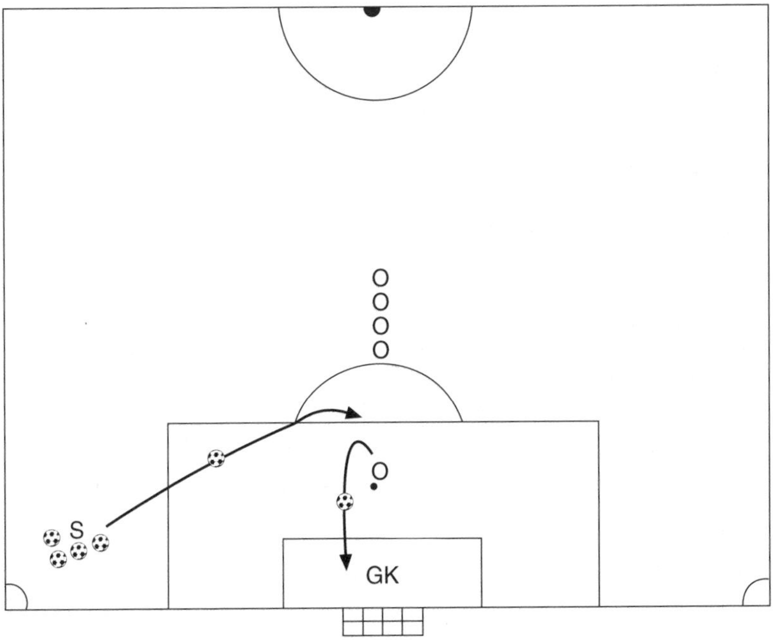

43 Crossing and Heading to Goal

Purpose

To work on crossing on the run, pulling the ball back, and heading

Organization

Players (10 to 12) form 2 lines near each touch line, 2 servers near each line with supply of balls, 4 attackers on top of the penalty area, a goalkeeper in the goal.

Procedure

1. The server passes the ball toward the end line.
2. The player at the front of the line runs onto the ball and crosses it into the center (preferably one touch).
3. Players in the middle make criss-crossing runs from outside of the penalty area and try to score on goal.
4. Alternate the side of the field for the cross after each turn.
5. Have players switch roles after 10 attempts. (Have each group move together: the players on the left go to the middle, the middle player moves to the right, and the right-side players go to the left side of the field.)

Key Points

To perform the cross on the run the player moves his or her body forward in one direction and kicks the ball with force in another. The placement of the nonkicking foot is vital. It should be alongside the ball when the player makes contact. The head should be steady, eyes fixed on the ball, and arms helping with balance. The upper body and shoulders should turn and face the intended direction of the cross.

The kicker should contact the ball with the inside of the foot near the arc around the big toe. Players should have a relaxed swing and make solid contact. They should drive the ball on a low trajectory, away from the goalkeeper, toward the head of an attacker.

The attackers in the center should vary their runs. They remain outside the area until a player is about to kick the ball. If contact is made with the head, the ball should be driven downward to the corner of the goal. The player jumps to meet the ball and snaps through with his or her back for power.

Variations

1. Add a defender in the penalty area.
2. Have the crosser cut the ball back, then send it into the middle.

Crossing and Heading to Goal

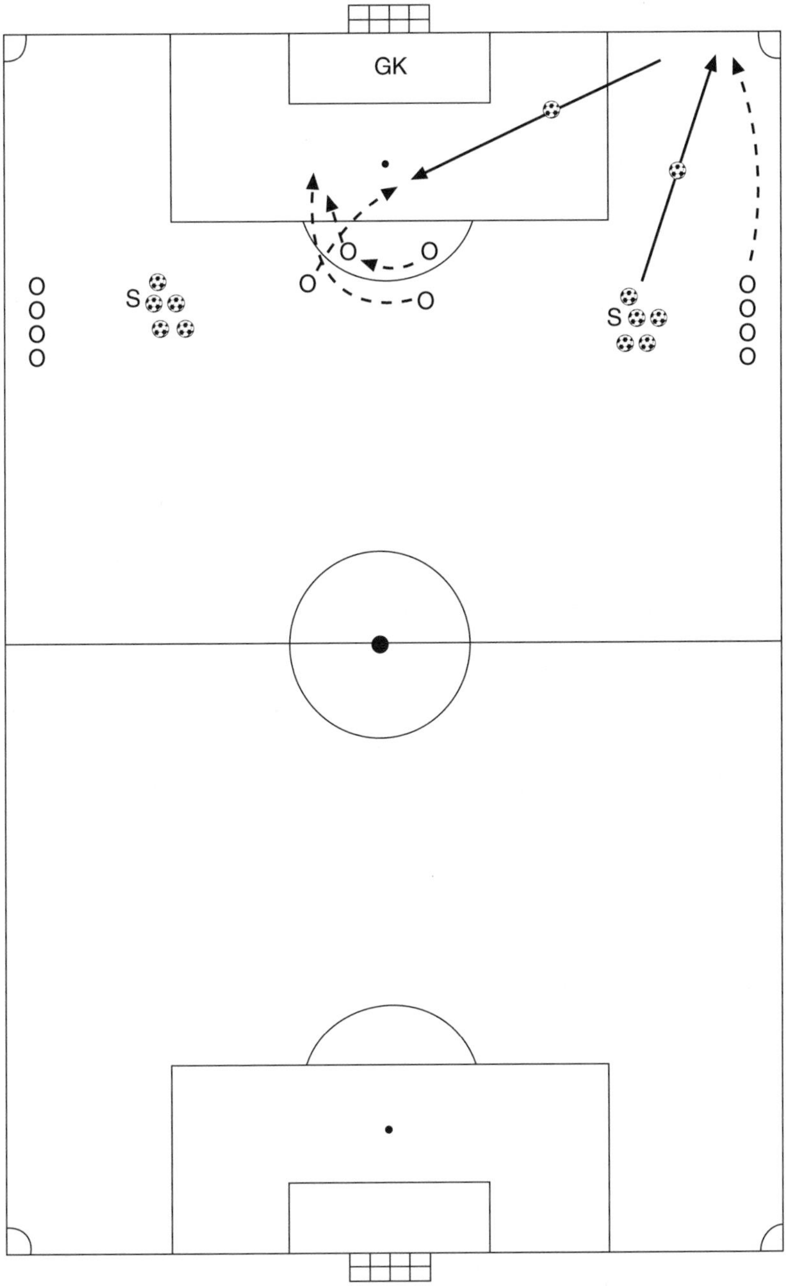

44 Bending a Pass or Shot

Purpose

To develop the ability to bend or curve the ball on a shot or pass

Organization

Set up on half the field. Players form 2 lines about 25 yards from the goal with a goalkeeper in the goal. Place 1 corner flag between each line and each goalpost to serve as obstacles between the ball and target.

Procedure

1. The first player in line places the ball in line with the flag and the goalpost, then tries to bend a shot around the outside of the flag and into the goal.
2. Alternate lines with each shot.
3. Have players experiment with contacting the ball with the inside and the outside of the foot.

Key Points

Bending the ball is an advanced skill. This type of kick is easier to perform on stationary balls and is useful for free kicks.

The bend is created by putting a horizontal spin on the ball. The foot making contact off the vertical center of the ball creates this spin. The follow-through does not extend to the target but off to an angle.

If the player wants to bend the ball inside the near post (from the right side of the field), he or she should contact the right side of the ball using the instep of the right foot or the outside of the left foot. The follow-through will extend in the direction outside of the post.

All the other techniques of shooting remain the same (head over the ball, stiff ankle, toe pointed down, watch the ball on contact, etc.). The only way for players to learn this skill is by developing a feel for it through continued practice.

Players can swerve a moving or a stationary ball. The farther from the vertical center and the nearer the side of the ball, the more the ball will spin. The steeper the angle of the foot and the more the toe is pointed down, the faster the ball will travel.

Variations

1. Have players try to bend a moving ball (they shoot while dribbling).
2. Change the positions of the shooters and the flags. Experiment with bending balls into the far post.
3. Have players try to bend shots off volleys.
4. Have players practice in pairs with a marker or other obstacle in between.

Bending a Pass or Shot

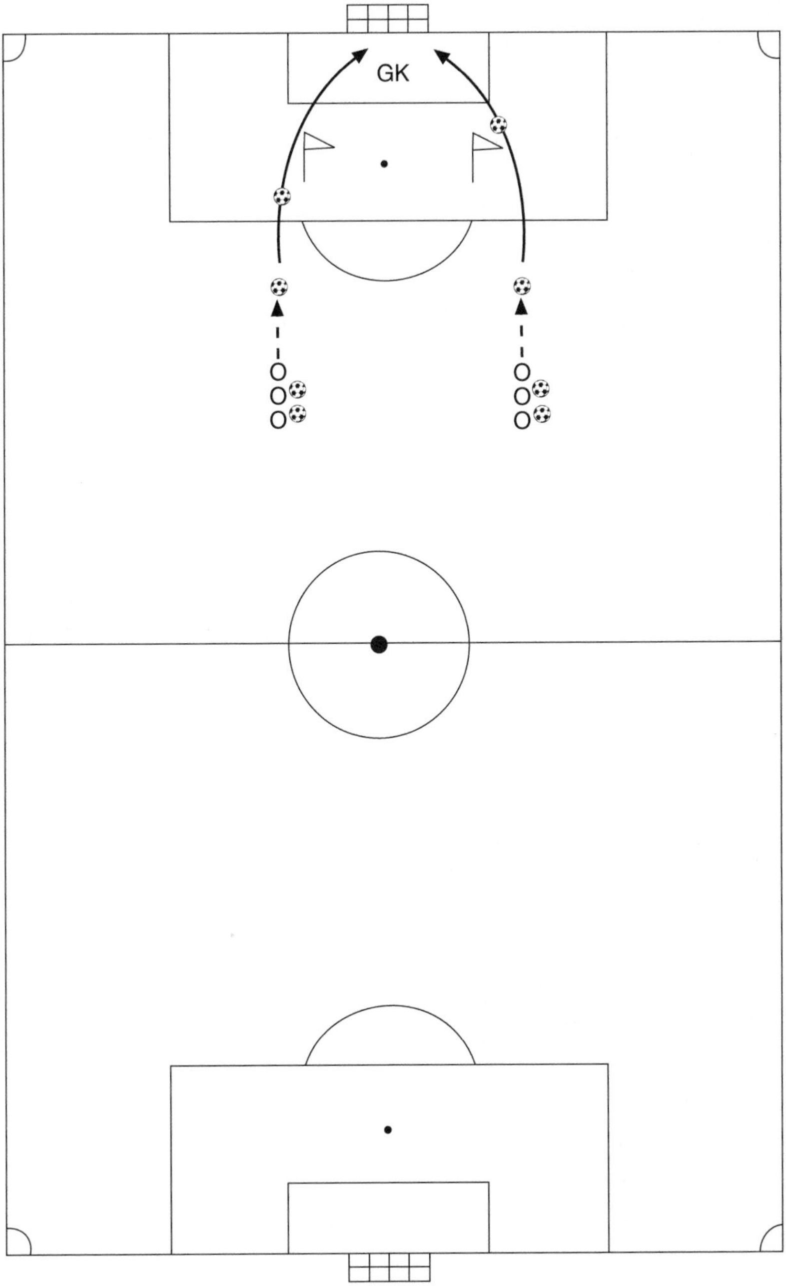

45 Shooting on the Turn

Purpose

To practice shooting around a defender, volleying

Organization

Form 2 lines, 1 goalie, 1 line of players with balls 30 yards out from goal, 1 line of defenders on the goal line. Duplicate setup with another goal if more than 4 players per line.

Procedure

1. The first player in the line runs to the penalty spot, checks back toward the line, receives a pass from the next person in line, turns, and shoots.
2. A defender starts on the goal line and races toward the player once the initial pass is made.
3. Players rotate positions after each turn.

Key Points

When a player is in scoring range, defensive pressure is usually at its height. Often the attacker will have a small window of opportunity to get a shot off. Encourage players in this exercise to shoot quickly. They will need to evaluate the position of the defender and the goalkeeper before the ball is received. To do this they will have to glance over their shoulder.

Players should try to shoot in one touch. As a player reaches the ball, the plant foot pivots, the body turns, and the ball is kicked. Players can use a second touch if necessary. With the first touch the player can turn the ball and pivot the body to face the goal with the ball. The ball is carried or pushed with the outside of the foot as the pass is received.

Variation

Have players practice shooting off the volley. The next person in line starts play by throwing the ball over his or her head or to the side of the shooter (defenders optional).

Shooting on the Turn

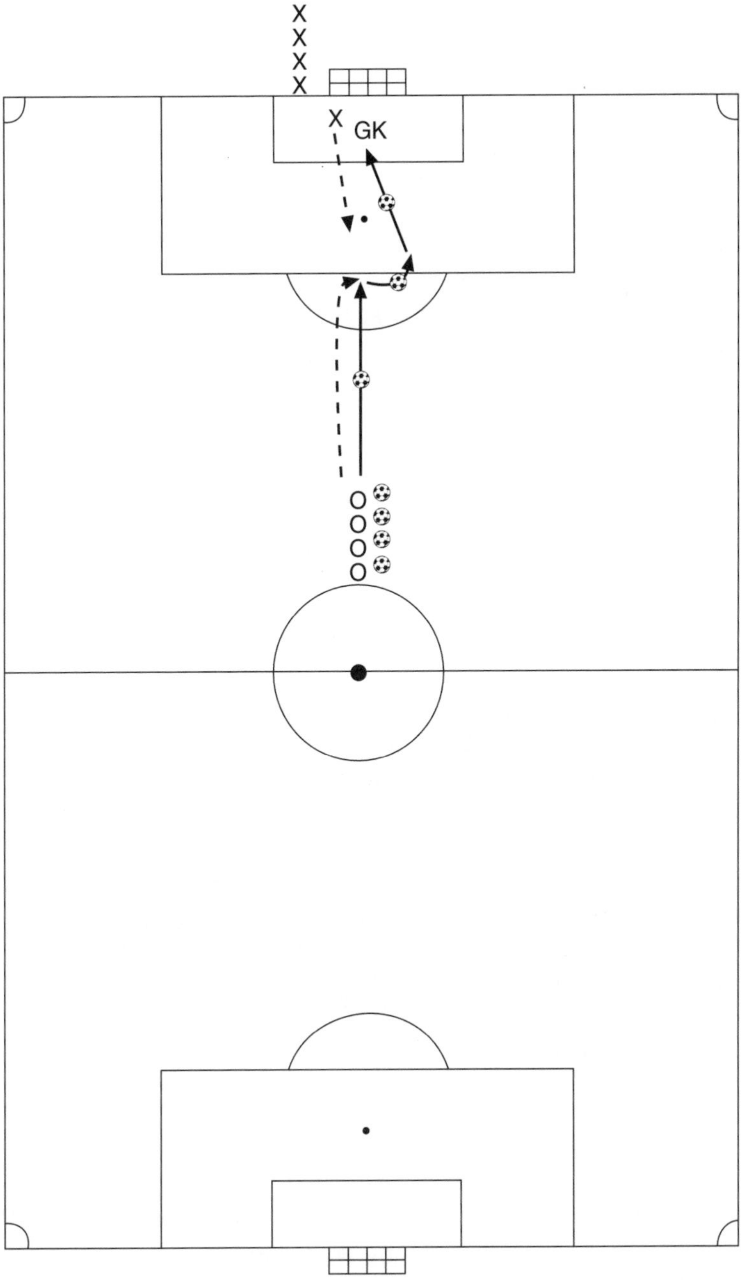

46 Side Volleys

Purpose

To practice volleying balls above knee height

Organization

Players pair up and face each other 7 to 10 yards apart as in *a*, 1 ball per pair.

Procedure

1. One player throws the ball up in the air to the side and volleys it to his or her partner (shown in *a*). The player should strike the ball when it is between waist and knee height.
2. Have players experiment with contacting balls on the fall and on the rise (after a bounce). Then have players try the following:
   a. Toss the ball to the side of the partner, who side volleys it back.
   b. Form two lines, one on each corner of the penalty area (see *b*), and have players try to side volley on goal. A server throws balls in front of the first player in line as he or she advances. The server alternates throws to each line. Have players switch lines after each turn.

Key Points

The side volley is a hard skill to perform but it might be the only chance for good contact when the ball comes in above knee height.

As the player prepares to strike the ball, the upper body must fall away from the ball. Doing this allows the hip to flex and gives the kicking foot sufficient room to swing through the ball. By dropping the shoulders, the player's head is still over the ball. (The head, shoulders, and ball are still in line, as when kicking a ball on the ground.)

The follow-through should continue downward across the body. Have players try to shoot the ball down and contact the ball above its horizontal midline with the instep. Timing, balance, and concentration are required to execute this skill effectively.

Variations

1. Instruct players to make the ball hit the ground after the volley, before it gets to the partner.
2. Use the same arrangement to practice volleys and drop volleys.
3. Start with one player facing the goal. A player standing behind throws the ball over the shooter's head; the shooter volleys the ball one touch.

Side Volleys

46

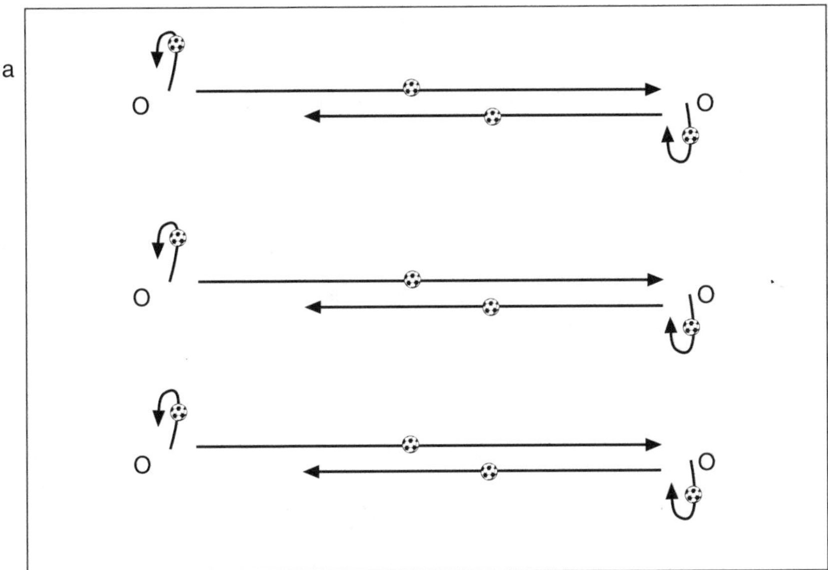

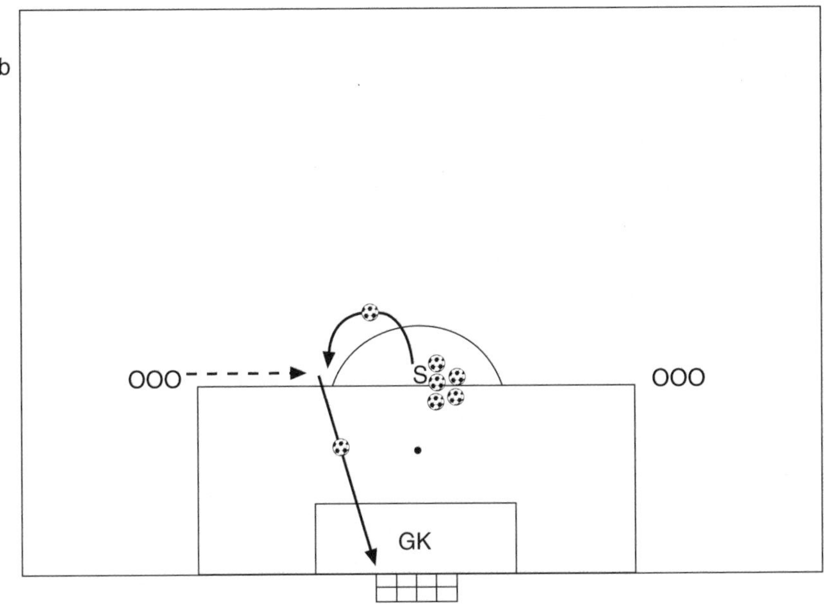

Controlling Balls Above Knee Height

Purpose

To work on controlling the ball with the thigh and chest traps

Organization

Use 5 to 14 players, 2 servers with a supply of balls near midfield, 1 line of players between servers, 1 target player at top of penalty area, a goalkeeper.

Procedure

1. The server plays a high ball into target player.
2. The target player controls the pass and lays it off to the attacker coming in for a shot (the person at the front of the line).

Key Points

The server should deliver a ball above the waist of the target player. This player will need to move into the flight path of the ball and try to cushion the force. The player performs the thigh trap by contacting the ball with the muscular part of the leg above the knee. The upper leg rises no more than parallel with the ground, then collapses as the ball hits.

The player performs the chest trap by absorbing the force of the ball while quickly leaning back on contact. The ball hits the chest then falls to the ground where it can be played with the feet.

Variations

1. Have a defender play behind the target player (passive defense at first).
2. Have the target player turn and shoot.
3. Alter the position of the servers so players can experiment with different angles of approach to the ball.

Controlling Balls Above Knee Height

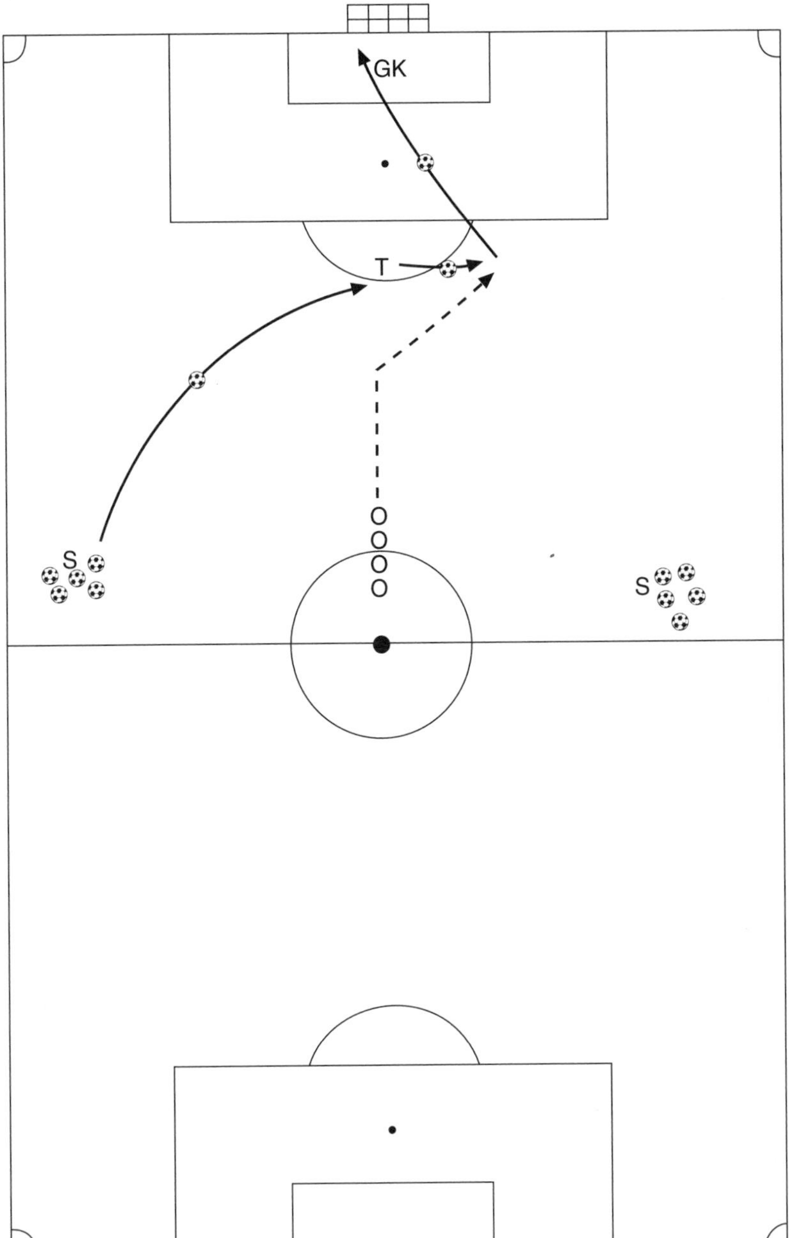

48 Offensive Heading

Purpose

To develop different heading techniques

Organization

Use 8 to 22 players, 1 line of players at midfield, 1 line of players (each with a ball) on the sideline, 1 line just outside the penalty area, a goalkeeper.

Procedure

1. Player O_1 runs toward the thrower (O_2) to receive a throw-in.
2. O_1 heads the ball back to O_2, who has entered the field.
3. O_2 controls the ball and passes it to O_3, who has run from the midfield into the corner.
4. O_1 loops back around the line and receives a cross from O_3.
5. O_1 heads the ball on goal.

Key Points

All the fundamentals of heading the soccer ball apply. Have players watch the ball and make contact with the forehead. Even though there are no opponents in this exercise, players should jump to meet the ball. For power the back is drawn back quickly (after the jump) then snaps forward as the head contacts the ball.

Useful sayings for players to visualize this movement include "grab the handlebars" or "throw your eyes at the ball." As with all heading, the eyes should be open and contact should be made with the forehead.

For this drill to succeed, accurate throw-ins and crosses are needed. These too are advanced skills.

Variation

Vary the position of the lines. Perform different passing combinations after the throw-in.

Offensive Heading

GK

OOO

O_1

O_3

OOO_2

OOO

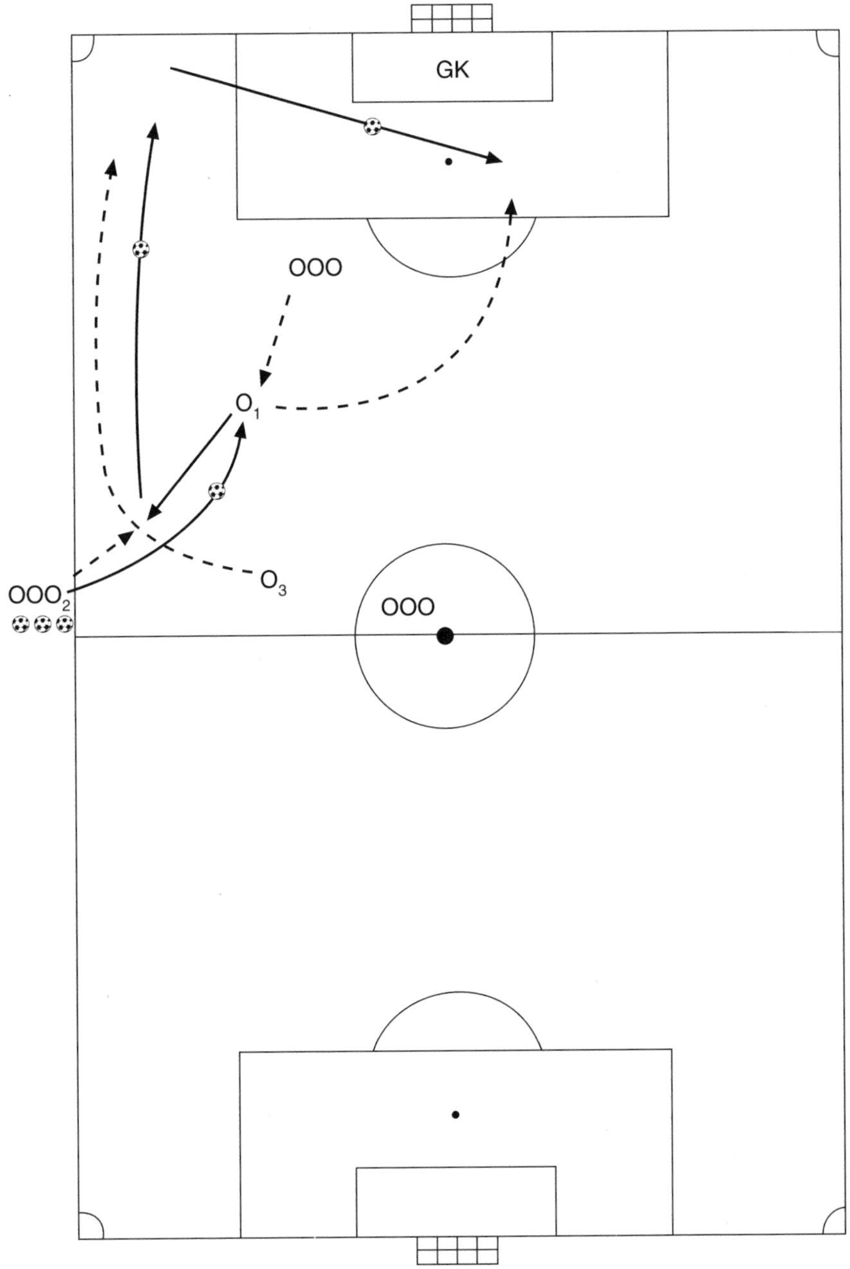

49 Defensive Heading

Purpose

To practice clearing the ball away from goal

Organization

Use 10 players, 2 wingers (crossers) in each corner with a supply of balls, 4 attackers (2 in penalty area, 2 outside the area), 4 defenders, a goalkeeper in goal.

Procedure

1. The wingers alternately cross balls into the penalty area.
2. The defenders head or volley the ball away from the goal.
3. If the defender fails to clear the ball out of the penalty area, the two additional attackers may enter the area and shoot on goal.

Key Points

The crossed ball is one of the most dangerous scoring opportunities. Defenders have to be able to challenge and win the ball in the air. The primary goal for the defenders in this situation is to contact the ball before the attackers do. If they can, they should head the ball with power and distance away from the goal.

Even if the attacker will likely get to the ball first, the defender should *go up* with him or her. Doing so will make it harder for the attacker to head to goal.

Variations

1. Add another attacker.
2. Extend the distance needed for cleared balls.

Defensive Heading

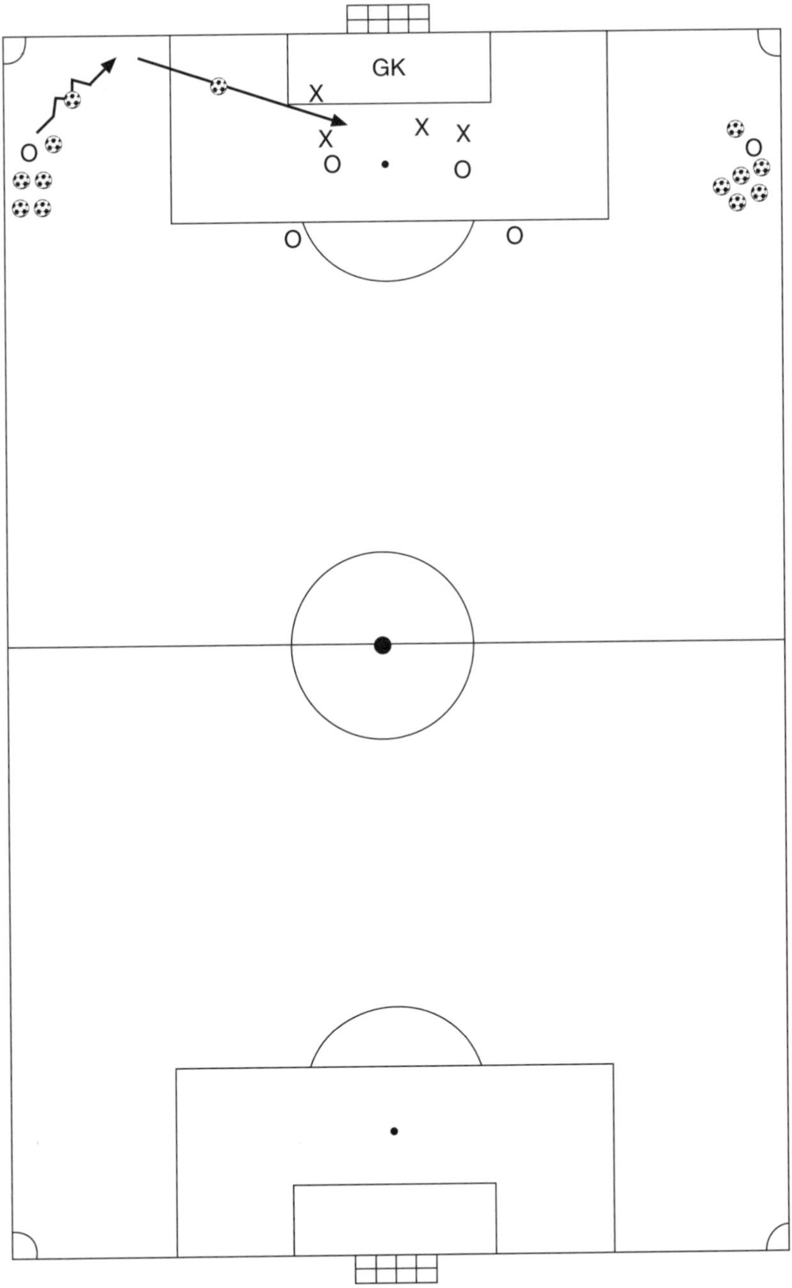

50 Heading Punts

Purpose

To practice winning long kicks, air balls

Organization

Position 6 to 8 players (in pairs) around the midfield line, 1 target player near the top of each penalty area, a goalkeeper with a supply of balls.

Procedure

1. Designate one player in each pair at the midfield line as offense, the other as defense.
2. The goalie starts by punting a ball toward any of the pairs.
3. The offensive player tries to head the ball to either target player; the defender tries to head the ball to the opposite target player.
4. Either player can try to settle or trap the ball off the punt.
5. Keep score. Have players switch roles after 10 attempts.

Key Points

More often than not, the goalkeeper is instructed to restart play by putting the ball down the field. Many teams leave winning the possession of the punt up to chance or defensive error. Players able to go up and win the punt can gain an advantage for their team by directing the ball to a teammate farther down the field or to one back in support.

When challenging for the punt, positioning is everything. Tell players to think that they are going to catch the ball (even have them try catching it a few times). They must be strong, determined, and confident when going up for the ball. The player should control the ball (not the other way around!).

Variations

1. Have players try to catch the ball with their hands (to work on proper positioning).
2. Play with two goalies, one in each goal, alternating punts.
3. Start play off a goal kick.

Heading Punts

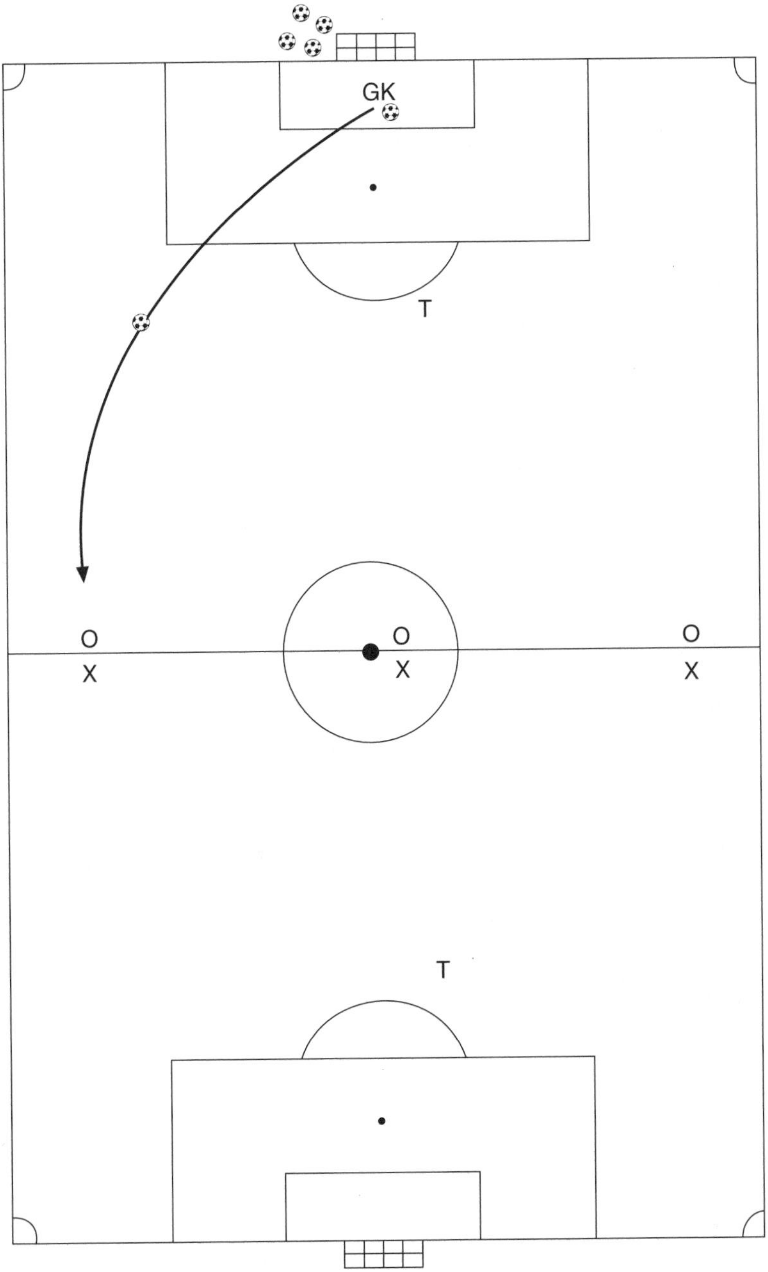

51 Diving Headers

Purpose

To practice the technique for the diving header

Organization

Grid 8 yards by 10 to 15 yards; 4 players (2 teams of 2) per grid, 1 player from each team on opposite end lines, 1 player (a server) from each team on opposite sidelines with a ball.

Procedure

1. The server, starting on the sideline at the middle of the grid, throws the ball to his or her teammate who runs in from the end line.
2. The teammate contacts the ball off a diving header. (The player must take off before crossing the midline of the grid.)
3. A point is scored if the ball travels past the line (below the shoulders) on the opposite end of the grid. One player from the other team defends the line.
4. After the attempt, the other team takes a turn from the opposite direction. Play can continue rapidly. One team does not have to wait for the other team to set up. Players on each team take turns serving and heading.

Key Points

The player uses the diving header to contact a ball with force when it is out of kicking range. The dive forward and solid contact with the forehead propel the ball forward.

This exercise helps players with the timing of the dive. Players have different landing techniques, in part depending on the height of the dive and the forward momentum. To avoid injury, players should use the arms to help break the fall.

Variations

1. Alter the length and width of the grid.
2. Allow end-line players use of their hands to defend the line.
3. Try diving headers off a cross on to goal.

Diving Headers

51

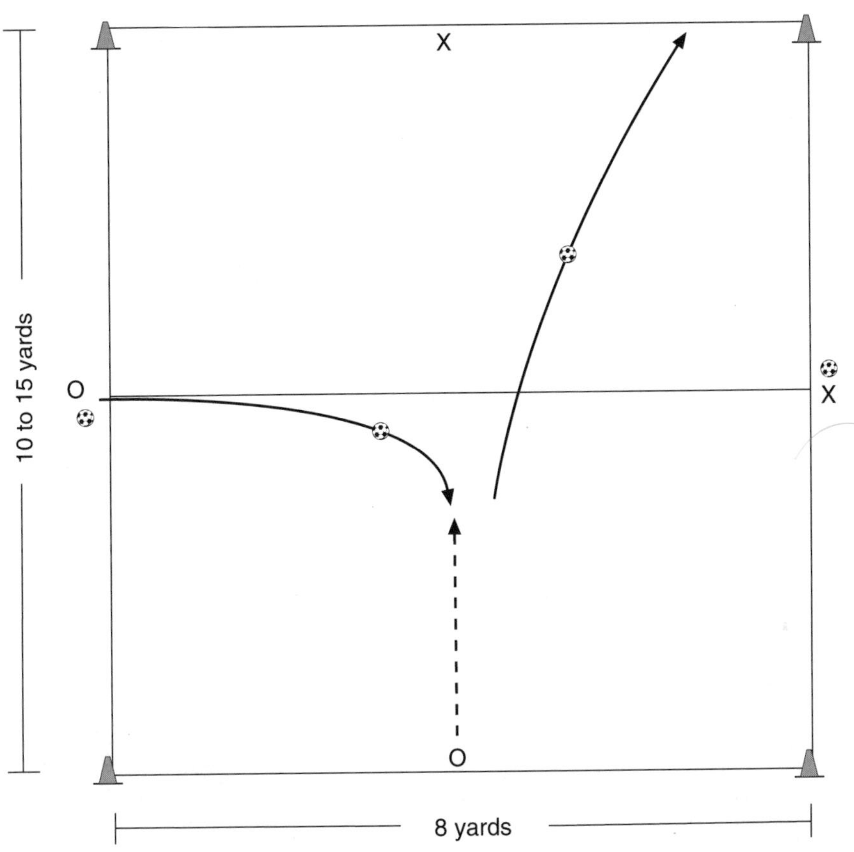

Courtesy of Indiana University/Guy Zimmer

CHAPTER 4

Fine-Tuning Team Play

Soccer is a team sport. Players work together to accomplish tasks and score goals. Individual skill is useless if the player is unable to benefit the objectives of the team.

Competitive teams try to coordinate efforts through tactical objectives. The primary objective of the game is to score more goals than the other team. Secondary objectives include maintaining possession of the ball and building up scoring opportunities.

This chapter is not so much a road map of tactical objectives as it is a tool for coaches to get players to think tactically. The drills ask that players have a reason for their actions. They create situations in which players work together with teammates to perform a task. Players will practice such things as marking opponents on a counterattack, maintaining ball possession until *positive play* is available, and building up scoring chances through the midfield.

Defensive pressure will vary as will the space and time allowed players to accomplish the tasks at hand. In games players will need to continually assess these factors to determine how to best serve the team. The drills in this chapter will help players create the mentality necessary for team play.

52 11 vs. 4

Purpose

To establish team shape and balance, to work on movement off the ball

Organization

Use 15 players. (11 players including a goalkeeper line up in position as if they are going to receive a punt or goalkick. Four defenders representing the opponent are positioned throughout the field. An additional goalkeeper can be in the opposite goal.)

Procedure

1. The team of 11 starts with the ball in the penalty area and advances the length of the field for a shot on goal.
2. If any of the four defenders win possession of the ball, the team of 11 restarts play from the penalty area.

Key Points

The emphasis of this exercise is balance. The team should be spread out, maintaining both depth and width. The player with the ball needs passing options and support from nearby players.

In some instances it takes imagination, discipline, and patience for the ball to be played up the field. As players pass and move off the ball, teammates will have to adjust.

Variations

1. Add two or three defenders who enter play from the opposite end line once the ball crosses midfield.
2. Set time limitations for advancing the ball.
3. Require that every player touch the ball before a shot can occur.
4. Put into effect a one- or two-touch restriction.
5. Require overlaps or other passing combinations.

11 vs. 4

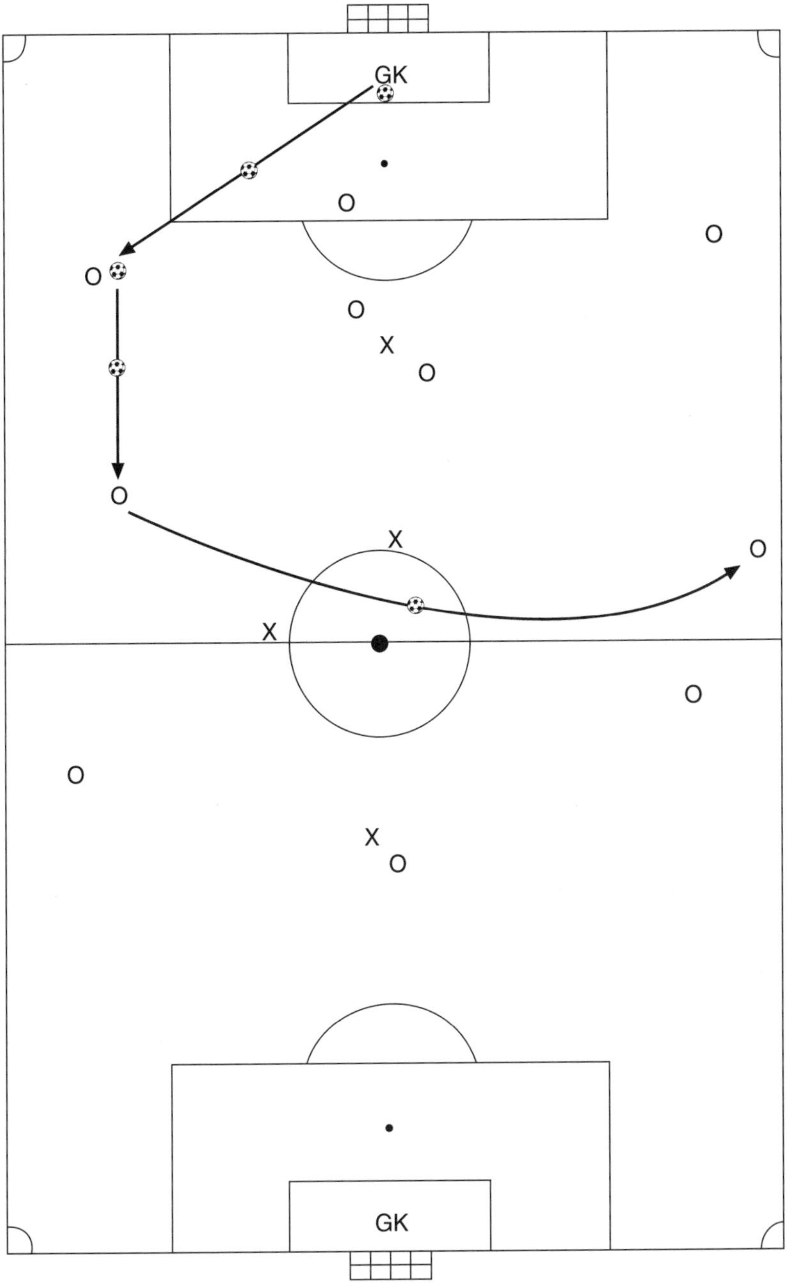

53 Possession Game (5 vs. 5 Plus 2)

Purpose

To practice quick passing, moving off the ball

Organization

Grid 20 to 30 yards by 30 to 40 yards; 12 players (5 per team, 2 neutral).

Procedure

1. The game is 5 vs. 5 keep-away with the addition of two neutral players.
2. The neutral players are always on offense. They play with the team that has possession of the ball.
3. Award a point if a team completes 10 passes in succession.

Key Points

This exercise emphasizes many skills necessary for advanced play—ball control, quick passing, ball movement, and vision. Two offensive players should move into close support of the player with the ball. Other teammates should spread out in the grid and take defenders away from the ball.

As defenders near the ball and cut off options, the other defenders should adjust. The one or two defenders near the ball don't have to win possession, they should focus on directing the play and cutting off passing options.

Variations

1. Change the size of the grid. A smaller grid will make the drill more difficult.
2. Require one or two touches per player.

Possession Game (5 vs. 5 Plus 2)

O X O
X
O
N
X
X N X
O
O

30 to 40 yards

20 to 30 yards

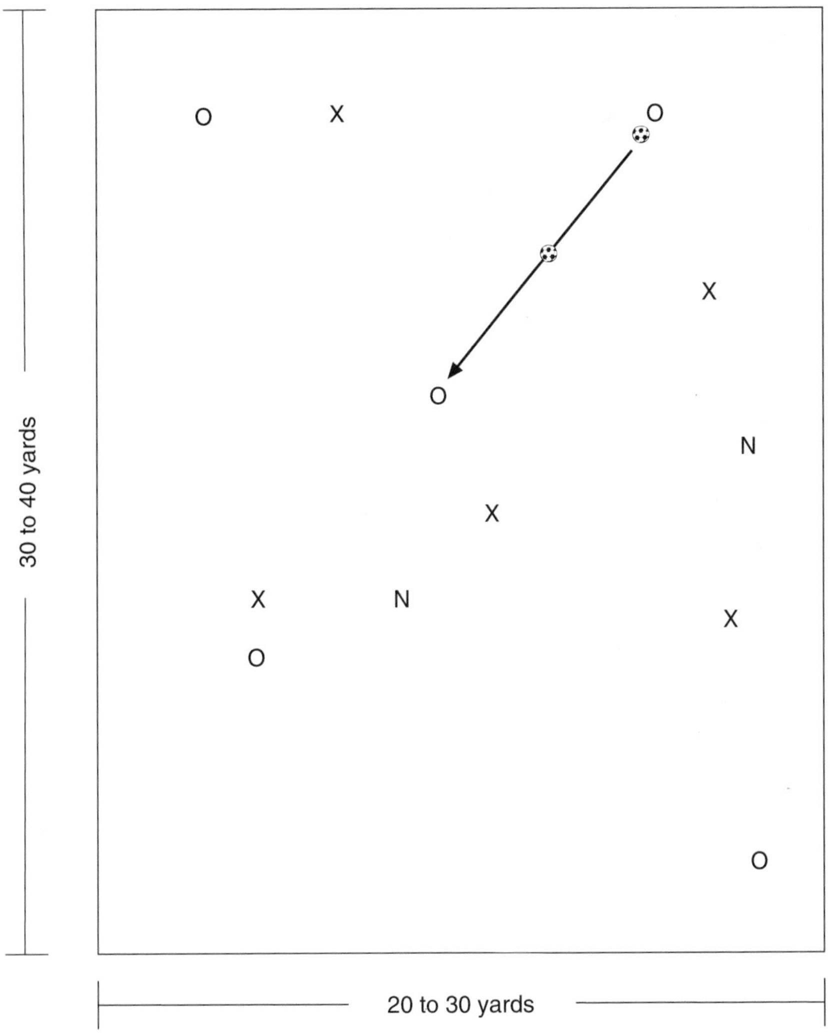

54 Last Goal Wins

Purpose

To distinguish between playing for possession versus playing to penetrate to goal

Organization

Use 8 to 20 players (2 teams with goalkeepers set up for a regular scrimmage).

Procedure

1. Play a regular scrimmage except that when a team scores it cannot score again until after the other team scores.
2. Play for a predetermined time (10 minutes). The last team to score wins.
3. The goalkeeper can become an extra field player for the team trying to score.

Key Points

After one team scores, the game takes a dramatic change. The scoring team tries to maintain possession, while the other team attacks all out. Players will experience the difference of possession soccer versus penetration soccer. In possession soccer the primary objective is to find support players with little or no defensive pressure. When penetrating to goal, teams willingly risk losing the ball to create scoring chances.

Variation

Allow a team to score a second time after completing 10 consecutive passes.

Last Goal Wins

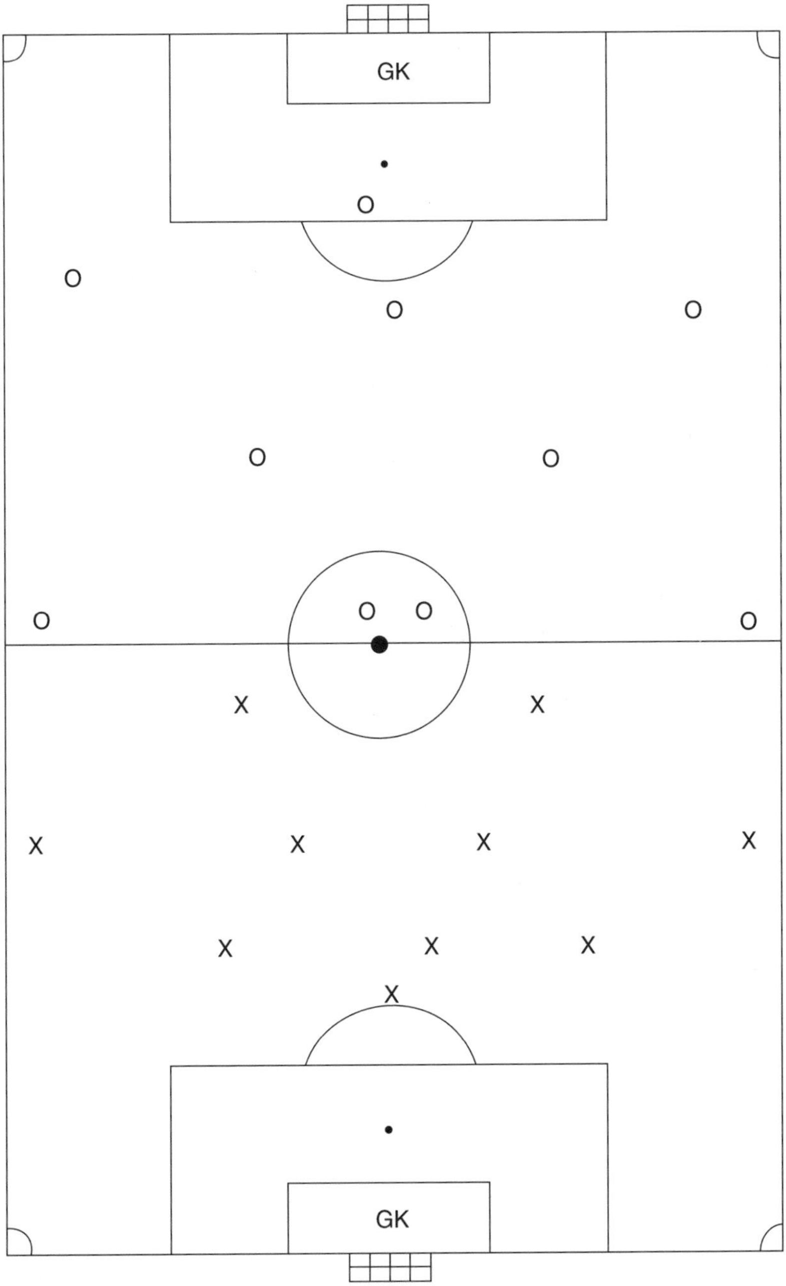

55 Keep-Away With Target Player

Purpose

To determine when to play for possession versus playing to move the ball up the field

Organization

Grid 20 to 25 yards by 30 to 35 yards, 8 to 14 players, 2 teams in grid, 1 target player on each end line.

Procedure

1. Each team tries to complete five passes in the grid, then pass to a target player at the end of the grid.
2. For a point to count, the player on the end of the grid must complete a pass back to a teammate inside the grid.
3. If the team maintains possession they try to advance the ball to the target player on the other end line.

Key Points

Players should keep possession of the ball by playing sideways or backwards until they can play it forward. The second attacker—the player closest to the ball—should be in a position of support square or behind if the player with the ball is being pressured by a defender. Whenever possible the ball should be played forward.

Have players look for passing combinations. Are they keeping a balance to the field? Are players adjusting freely? If one runs forward, does another fall back and cover the space?

Variation

Restrict the end-line player to one or two touches.

Keep-Away With Target Player

T

30 to 35 yards

T

20 to 25 yards

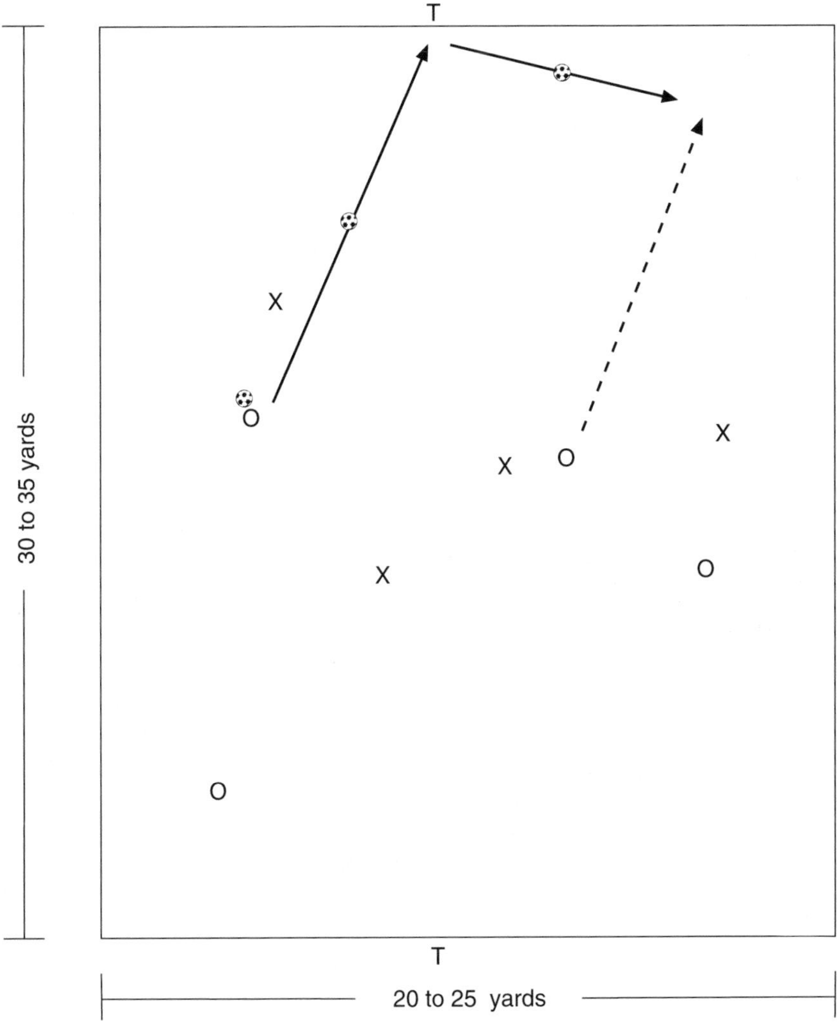

56 Runs From the Back

Purpose

To practice attacking from the back, using the space on the wing

Organization

Use 5 players (3 players at midfield, 2 attackers in the middle); a goalkeeper.

Procedure

1. Play starts by three players passing on the wing near midfield. Player O_2 should start deep and check toward the player with the ball (O_3).
2. After several short passes, player O_1 or O_3 should overlap with a quick sprint down the wing. The ball should be played into the space down the line.
3. The player runs onto the ball and crosses it into the center to the two attackers, O_4 and O_5.

Key Points

The overlap is a dangerous attacking play. The overlapping player causes a defender to give chase from up the field or the defense to adjust quickly to cover the open runner. Encourage midfielders and defenders to overlap if they can gain a clear advantage. In a game situation, other players will need to cover the space or opponents that are left open (should the other team win the ball and counterattack).

With a defender, as in the variation, the checking forward will need to create space on the side for the overlapping runner. The forward should try to lead the defender to the inside by running back at an angle (from the outside to the inside). The pass down the line may have to be lifted or curved depending on the position of the defender.

The cross in the center should be taken from near the end line and pulled back to the forwards who have timed their runs accordingly.

Variations

1. Add another defender who starts behind the deep forward on the wing.
2. Start play with a pass from the center of the field.
3. Change the starting positions of the three players on the wing.

Runs From the Back

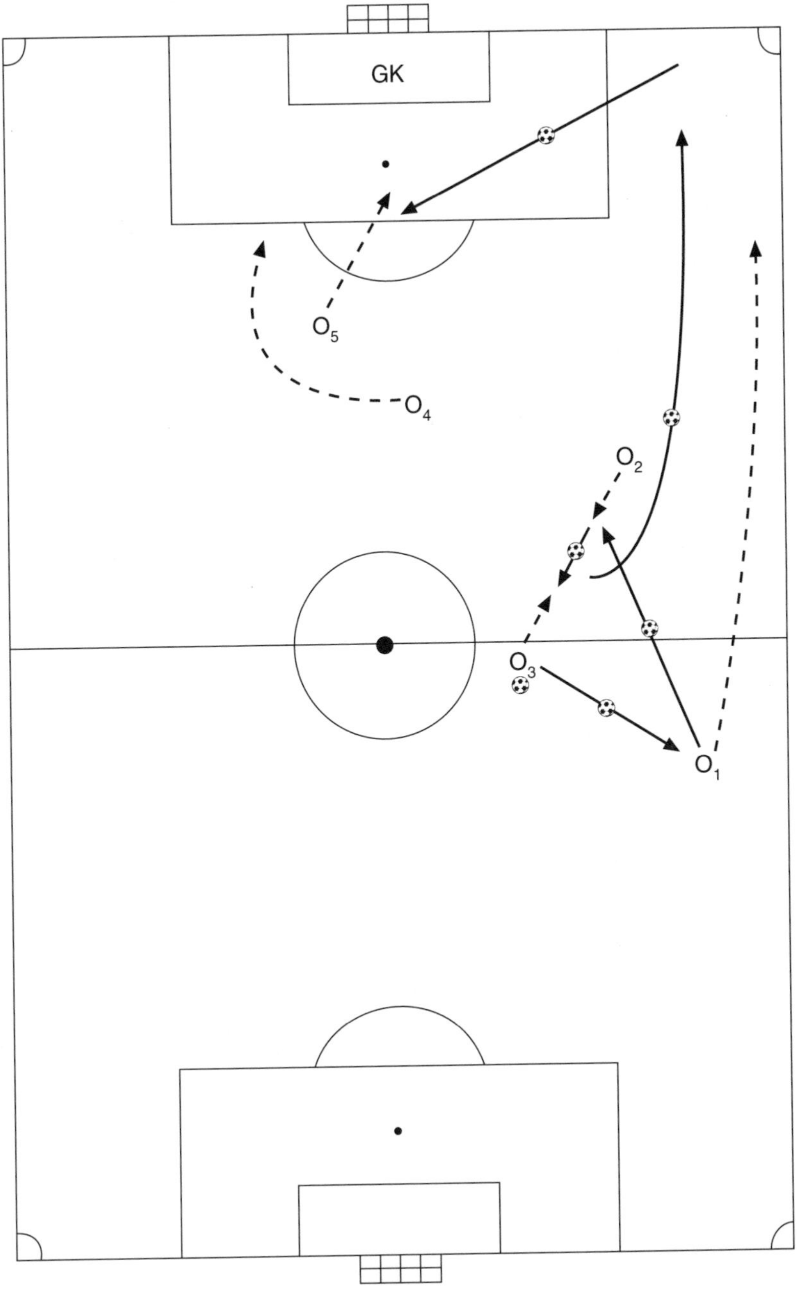

57 Point Player (3 vs. 1, 1 vs. 1)

Purpose

To practice making checking runs and keeping possession

Organization

Use 4 attackers, 2 defenders, 1 goalkeeper; 3 vs. 1 in a 10 by 10 yard grid near midfield, 1 vs. 1 at top of the penalty area.

Procedure

1. Three players keep the ball away from a defender. After five passes in the grid, they try to advance the ball to the attacking player who starts on the top of the penalty area.
2. The 1 vs. 1 players have to stay in the penalty area until the five passes have been completed.
3. After the pass forward all players can advance toward goal.

Key Points

Players link short passes to maintain possession as they wait for the right moment to advance the ball. When the pass is on, the attacking player will have to check toward the ball. The players in the grid will need to move quickly into supporting passing lanes. The attack, once on, should happen without delay.

Variations

1. Add players to make a 3 vs. 2, 2 vs. 2 situation.
2. Add another defender (or two) who enters play from the goal line after the five passes.

Point Player (3 vs. 1, 1 vs. 1)

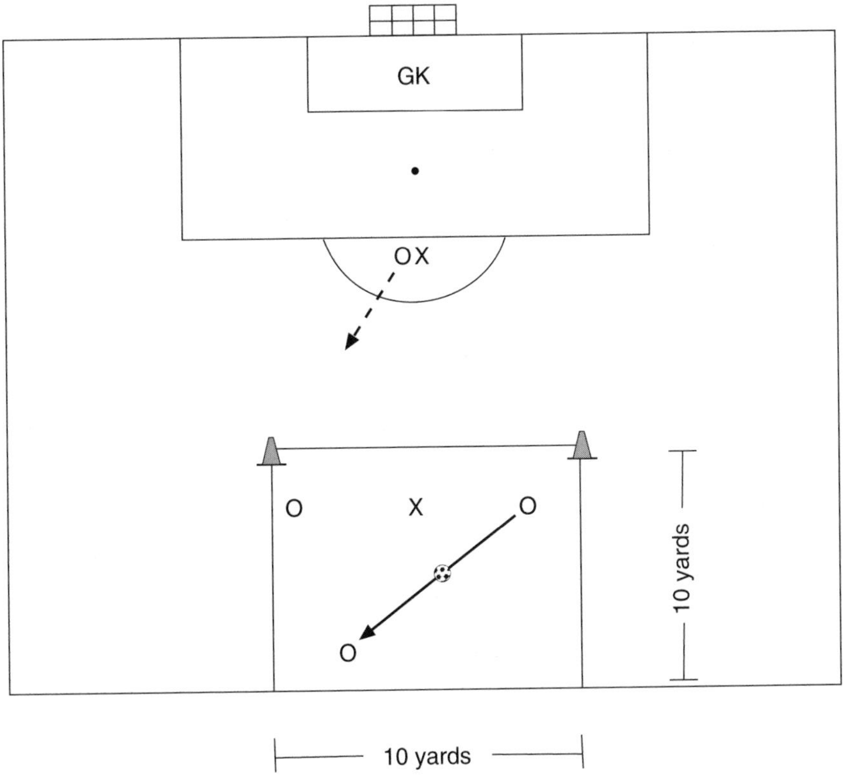

58 3 vs. 2, 3 vs. 2

Purpose

To work on combination passing to create scoring chances

Organization

Grid 20 by 30 yards with portable goals (if available) on each end, 10 players (2 teams of 5), 2 goalkeepers, 3 players from 1 team and 2 players from the other team in each half of the grid.

Procedure

1. Restrict players to their respective zones. Players try to advance the ball to teammates in the other half of the grid.
2. Offensive players try to score on goal. Play is restarted by a throw or kick from the goalkeeper.
3. If the other team wins the ball, play continues in opposite direction.

Key Points

This game isolates several tactical situations. Players will perform combination passes as well as take on defenders in 1 vs. 1 situations.

One defender will need to put immediate pressure on the ball. If a player has a shot at the goal, he or she should take it without delay.

When the side with three players has the ball, players in support should focus on their angle and distance of support in relation to one another. The angle should be square or behind square.

When the supporting players are allowed to cross the line (as in the variation), scoring chances will depend on the timing of the runs. They must anticipate the possibility of two- and three-player combinations.

Variations

1. Require the three defenders to start at the back of the grid until the pass forward is made.
2. Allow the back players to cross the midline.
3. Require shots from the far grid. Teammates in the near grid can play the rebound.
4. Play without goals (keep-away).

3 vs. 2, 3 vs. 2

58

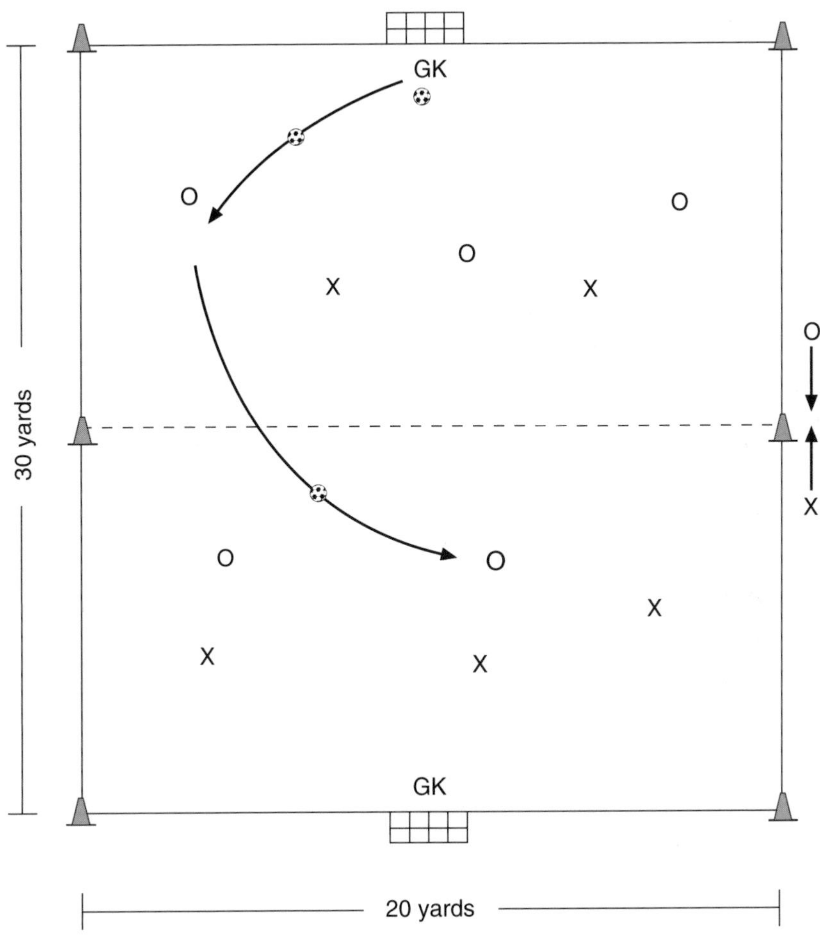

59 Hold the Line

Purpose

To practice defensive marking near the goal

Organization

Use 6 players per turn, 3 attackers and 3 defenders on top of the penalty area, a server with a supply of balls, a goalkeeper in goal.

Procedure

1. The server plays a ball into one of the attackers.
2. The receiving player tries to turn and shoot or pass to a teammate.
3. Defenders try to thwart attack, clear ball, or pass back to server.
4. Enforce the offside rule.
5. Rotate new players in after each turn.

Key Points

The offense is trying to get the ball into the space behind the defense. Most goals occur from this space. Attackers can turn and shoot if the defense isn't marking tightly, or the attacker can pass. The pass can be a quick combination or through pass past the defense.

The defensive priority is to stop the player receiving the ball from turning. Defenders have to be careful not to overcommit to the ball or the attacker, however. They need to play behind the attacker to be in a position to challenge a through pass.

Variations

1. To encourage shooting, start the defenders on the goal line.
2. Attackers must pass at least once before shooting.
3. Add another defender (sweeper).

Hold the Line

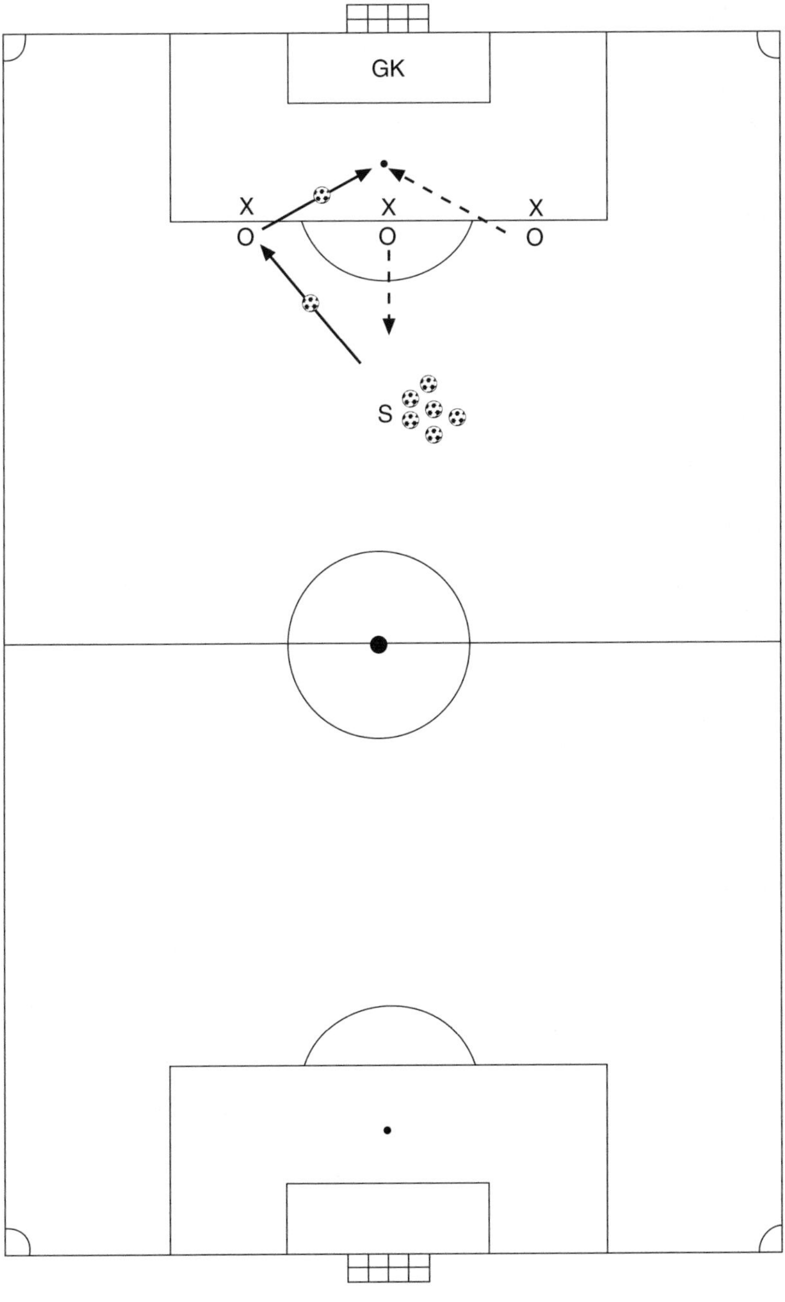

60 Boxed In (6 vs. 4, 3 vs. 3)

Purpose

To work on creating and defending scoring situations

Organization

Use 16 players (9 attackers, 7 defenders); 1 goalkeeper. Set up a 6 vs. 4 outside the penalty area, 3 vs. 3 inside.

Procedure

1. The six attackers outside the penalty area try to pass the ball to the teammates in the box.
2. The defenders try to clear the ball out and away from the goal.
3. The six attackers and the four defenders assigned to the outside of the penalty box are not allowed to enter it. The three offensive players and three defensive players are not allowed to leave the penalty area.

Key Points

The six offensive players outside the penalty area must pass wisely and should rarely force a pass that may result in a turnover. They have a two-player advantage. Two players should always be open. The pass into the box has to be good so the player outside the box has to have a reason to make the pass. Does the player receiving the ball have a momentary advantage? Is the marking defender out of position? Can the player play a one-touch pass to another attacker?

Players should look for give-and-go options in the variation in which all players can enter the box after the initial pass.

Variations

1. You can adjust the number of players on either team to emphasize different aspects of the drill. To increase offensive heading, for example, decrease the number of defenders or add attackers. Add a fourth defensive player (sweeper) in the penalty area to make it harder on the attackers.
2. Let players enter the penalty area after one of three offensive players in the penalty area touches the ball.

Boxed In (6 vs. 4, 3 vs. 3)

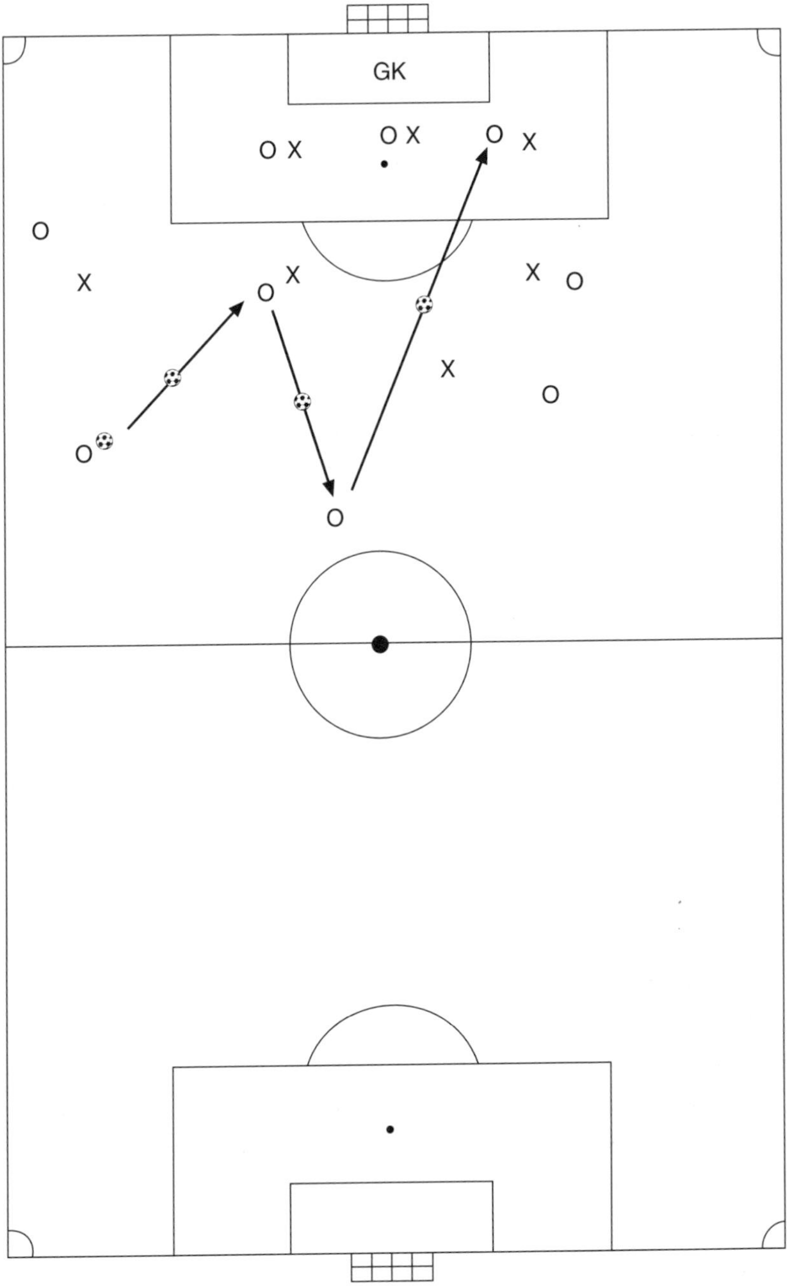

61 Defending the Penalty Area

Purpose

To practice defensive marking, clearing, and crossing

Organization

Use 11 players (5 defenders, 6 attackers); 1 player from each team on either wing; 3 defenders and 3 attackers in the penalty area; 1 attacker outside the penalty area; a goalkeeper; two servers near the sidelines with a supply of balls.

Procedure

1. Play starts on either wing with a server passing the ball to the space ahead of the offensive player.
2. The wing offensive player chases down the ball and tries to cross the ball into the center. If the defender is blocking the cross, the winger can pass it back to the supporting teammate on top of the penalty area.
3. Play continues until a shot on goal results or the defense clears the ball past the halfway line.
4. Keep score and analyze how the players score each goal.

Key Points

Defenders must challenge and win the ball when it enters the penalty area. If an attacker has the ball within shooting range, then defenders must apply immediate pressure. The defenders should hold a line together. They should push up and away from the goal quickly as a unit when the ball is cleared.

The wing player should take the cross one touch if space is available. If the defender has cut off the angle, the winger will need to cut it back. At this moment, the player can attempt another cross or pass the ball to the support player. The support player can continue play by dribbling or passing.

Variations

1. Server can vary the type of pass (to feet, to space, in the air).
2. Give the offensive player on the wing a two- or three-step advantage.

Defending the Penalty Area

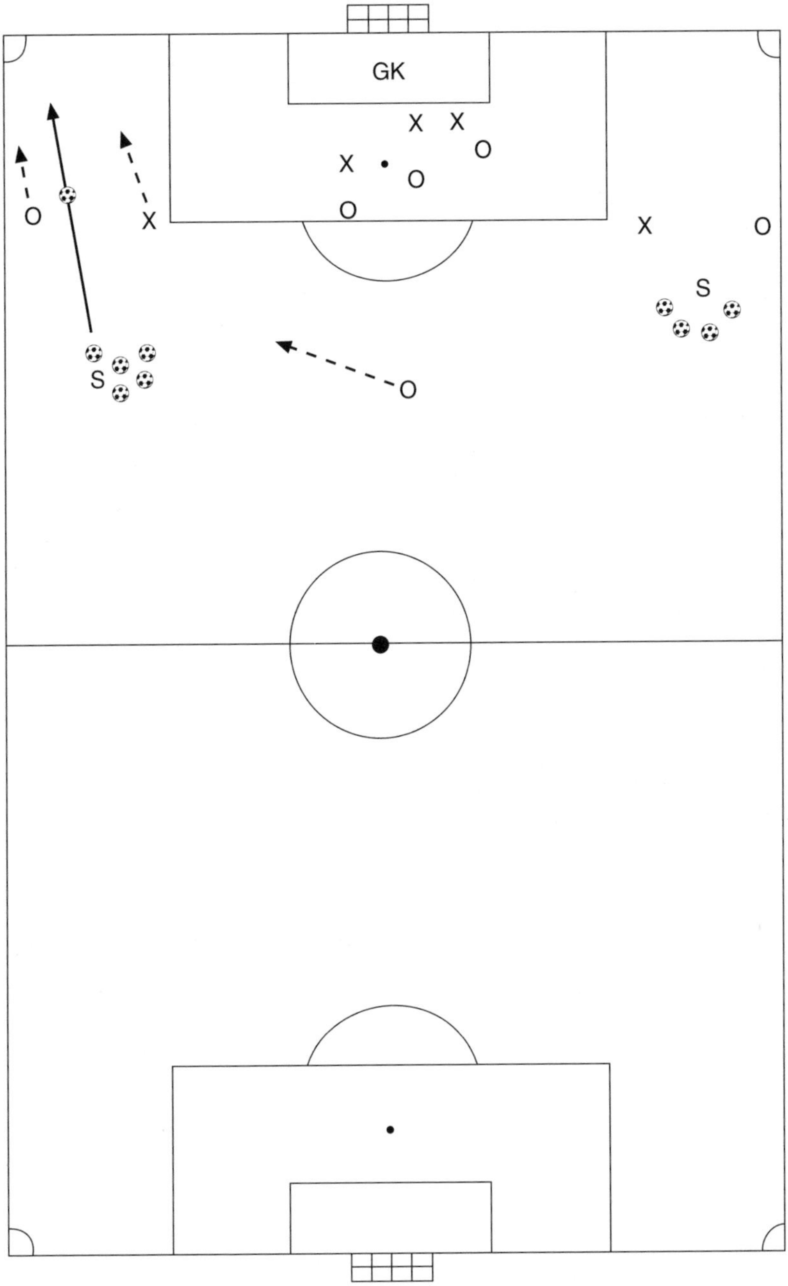

62 Throw-Head-Catch

Purpose

To practice heading with direction, moving to open space

Organization

Use 8 to 14 players (2 teams) on a field 20 by 30 yards with 2 full-size goals.

Procedure

1. Play starts by a player throwing the ball to a teammate.
2. This player heads the ball so that another teammate can catch it and restart the sequence (throw-head-catch).
3. If the ball hits the ground, award the other team possession and continue play in the other direction.
4. The defensive team can use the hands to intercept a ball or break up the play only after a headed pass. Play without goalkeepers.

Key Points

This game emphasizes movement off the ball and accurate heading. Players have to know where to direct the ball before it arrives. It is essentially a one-touch game. The player throwing the ball should not throw the ball to a teammate unless that player has someone else to head to. Encourage players not to rush if the play isn't on. In this game, players have the luxury of time.

Players also practice heading technique. The headed pass needs power along with accuracy.

Variations

1. Restrict players from heading back to the player who threw the ball.
2. Players throw the ball to themselves to head. The next player catches the ball then heads it to another teammate.
3. Players advance the ball by half volleying it out of their hands—catch, half volley, catch, half volley. Players can score on goal with a header only.
4. Play to end zone instead of goals.

Throw-Head-Catch

30 yards

X
O
X
O
X
O
X
O
X
O
X
O

20 yards

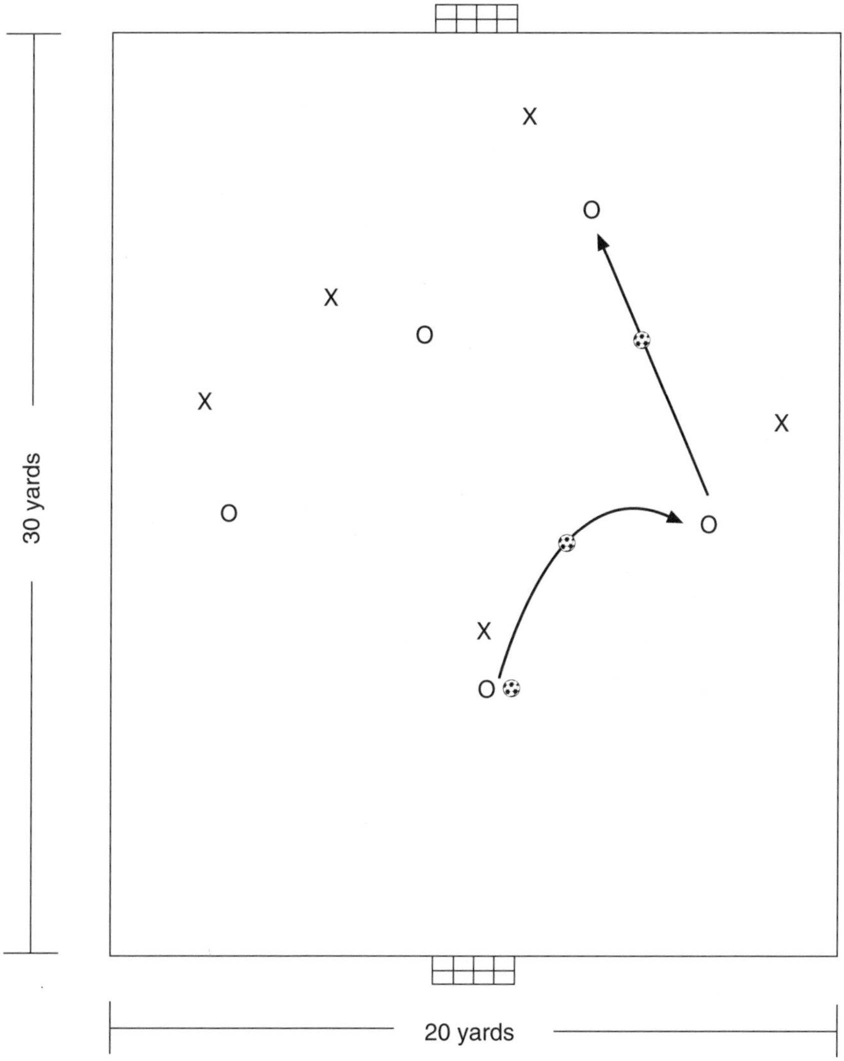

63 Counterattack

Purpose

To practice playing behind the defense, looking for the early cross or breakaway

Organization

Make 2 teams, 3 or 4 players each, use 1 goalkeeper. The teams line up on the midline; identify 1 team as offense, the other defense. Position 2 servers with a supply of balls at midfield near the sidelines.

Procedure

1. The server passes the ball into space toward the goal.
2. All the players from the two teams rush forward into the space. The defenders try to thwart the attack and return the ball to the midfield; the offense tries to score on goal.
3. Enforce the offside rule.

Key Points

The objective for the offense is to attack before the defense can get set up. The server can play a long ball into space or link a shorter pass to an open attacker. Either way, play must continue forward quickly.

The early cross is usually wasted on the far post. The player should deliver it toward the near post, over and behind the defenders, curling back toward the incoming forwards. The center attacker should be running in at near full speed on a diagonal. It is most effective if delivered before the defenders can set up.

Variation

Allow one defensive player (the sweeper) and one forward to start at the top of the penalty area. Play can start with a pass to the forward.

Counterattack

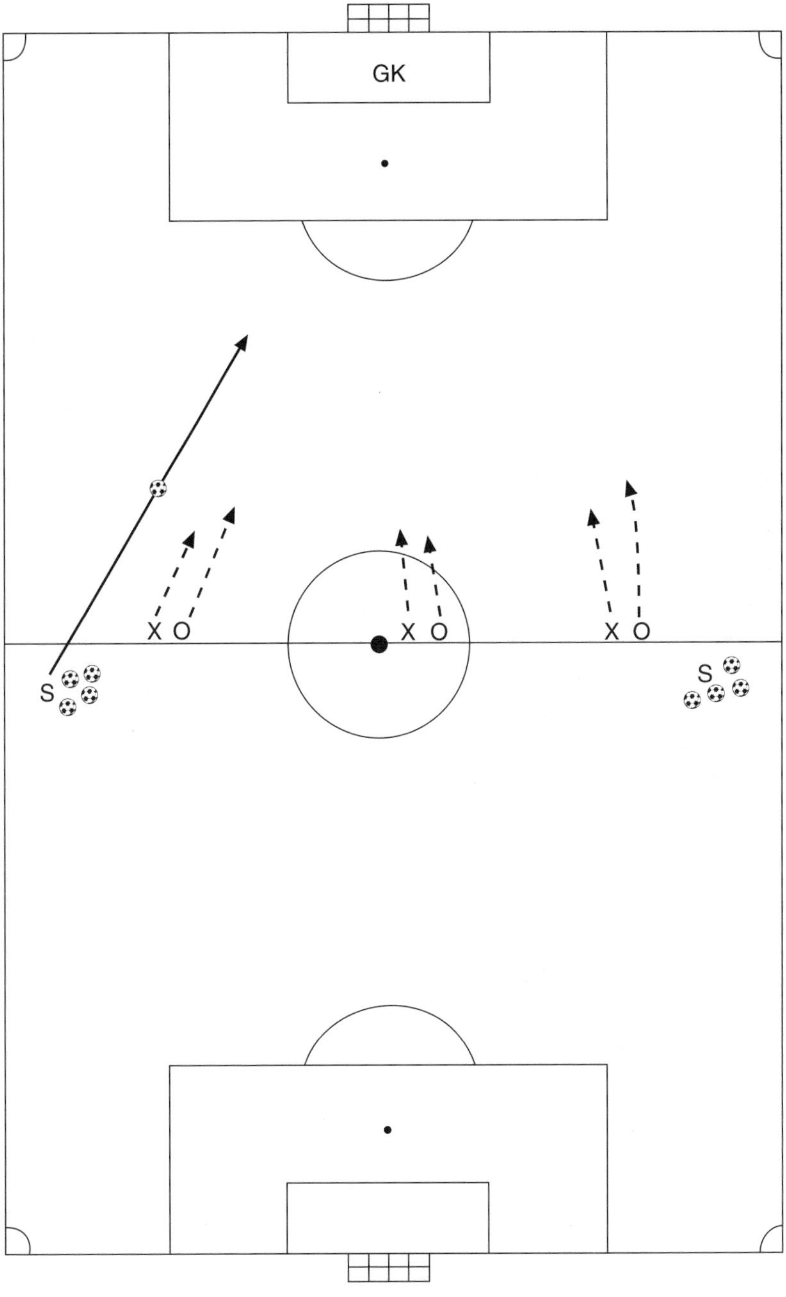

64 Midfielder With Space

Purpose

To practice creating scoring opportunities, committing a defender

Organization

Use 10 to 16 players; 2 teams of 3 players each in the penalty area; 1 line of players with balls near midfield; 1 extra defensive player, the target player, positioned near the midfield line; 1 goalkeeper in goal.

Procedure

1. The player at the front of the line dribbles toward goal. At this moment the six players can leave the penalty area.
2. The midfielder can continue dribbling or pass the ball at any time.
3. If the defense wins the ball they try to pass it to a target player near the midfield line.
4. Switch the role of the players after a goal is scored or the ball is cleared to the target player.

Key Points

This attacking situation is fairly common in games. The forwards are marked tightly; the midfielder has time and space to advance. The midfielder can dribble straight to the goal if not picked up by a defender. The forwards should stay spread out to make it difficult for the defenders to mark. As the dribbler nears, one of the defenders will have to pressure the ball and leave open an attacker. This attacker should get in a position to receive a pass before the defender tackles the dribbler.

The forwards can turn and shoot if they get the ball or play it back to the midfielder.

Variations

1. Add a sweeper; play the offside rule.
2. Vary the starting position of the ballcarrier (e.g., have the line start on the side of the field).

Midfielder With Space

GK

OX XO XO

T

O
O
O
O

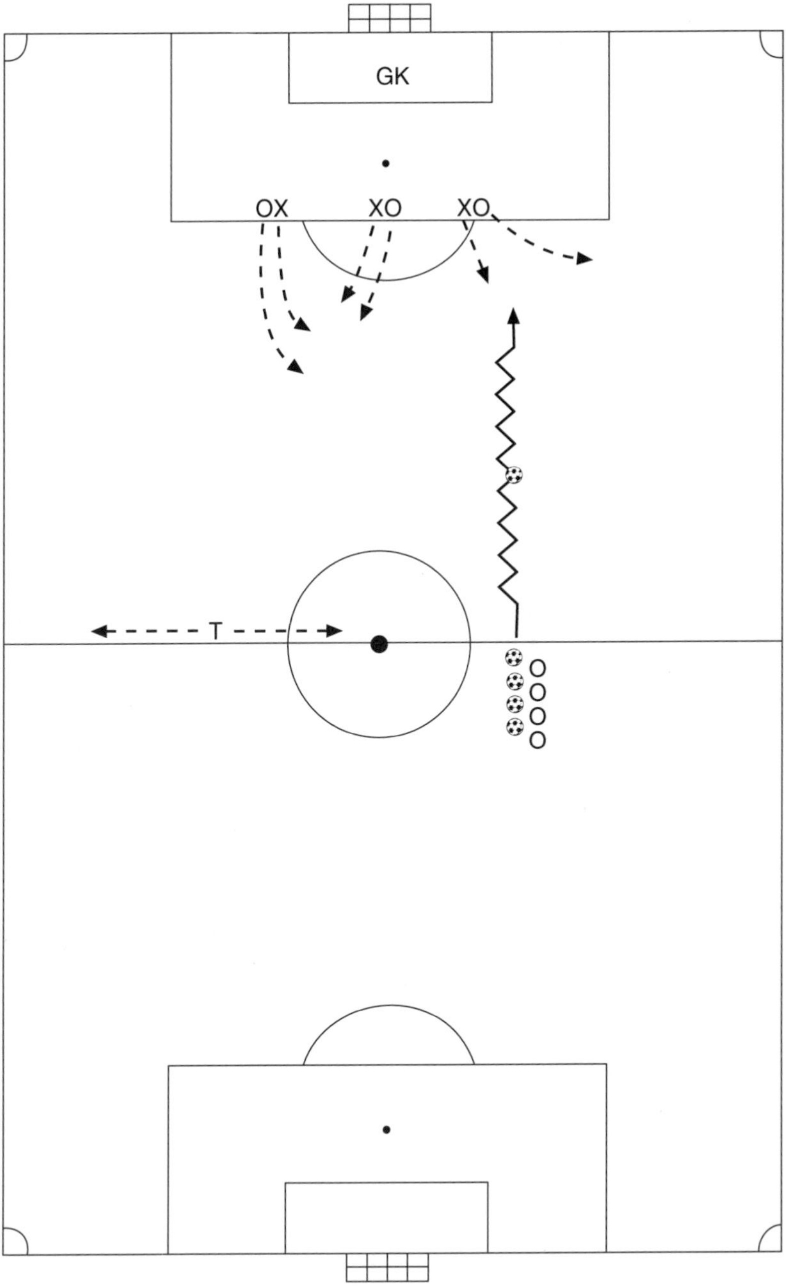

65 Through Ball, Early Cross

Purpose

To attack quickly with a numbers up situation.

Organization

Use 10 or more players; 1 group of players plays 5 vs. 2 (or 3 vs. 1) in grid 15 by 15 yards near the midfield. Start 2 lines of attackers near the center of the field; 2 defenders mark the first 2 players in line.

Procedure

Play starts with players in the grid completing five consecutive passes. When they complete the passes all players, including the attackers at the front of the line, can advance toward goal. A through ball to the near runner can be played (diagonally toward the near post) or the ball can be crossed over the field to the far attacker.

Key Points

The defense is outnumbered. They will scramble to address the most immediate threat to goal. The offensive players in the 5 vs. 2 grid should advance the ball as quickly as possible after accomplishing the consecutive passes. The quicker the attack from this moment, the less time the defense has to set up and cover.

A diagonal, through pass to the near attacker is a dangerous attacking play (especially if the runner is even with or ahead of the marking defender). A cross, over the defense to the far side of the penalty area, is another option that can be played at any time during the attack. The defender marking the far attacker will have to drift inward to cover the extra attackers coming into play from the grid.

If the far runner receives the ball he or she can go to goal or pull the ball back toward the penalty spot. This play, the byline, produces good scoring opportunities. The runs into the box from supporting attacking players have to be timed to the moment the ball is played back from the end line.

Variation

Start with one or two additional defenders at the top of the penalty area.

Through Ball, Early Cross

15 yards

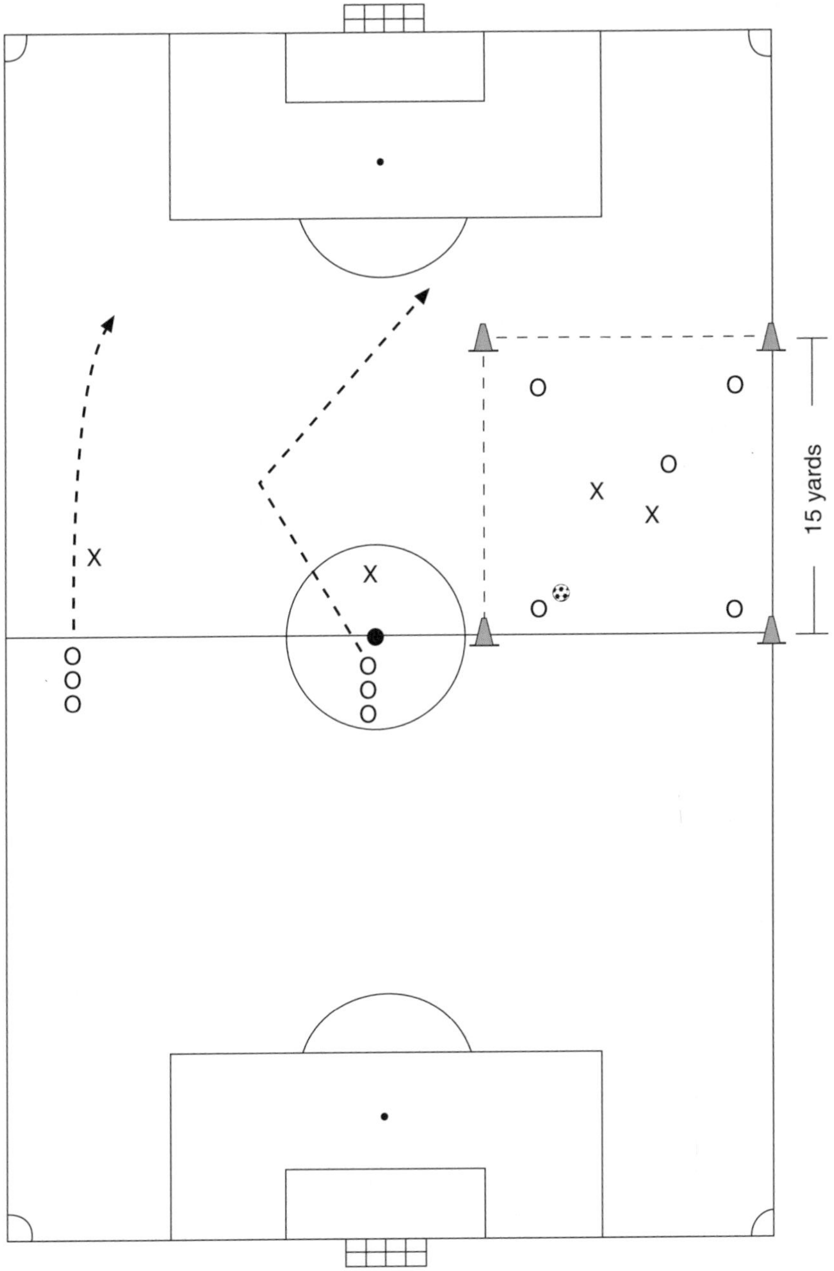

66 Defending the Pass (3 vs. 5)

Purpose

To practice shutting down passing options, channeling the direction of play

Organization

Grid 15 by 20 yards; 8 players (5 offense, 3 defense). All players start in the grid.

Procedure

1. Five offensive players play keep-away from the three defenders.
2. The offensive players are allowed only three touches before they must pass the ball.
3. Don't allow defenders to tackle the ball (at first). They can only intercept passes.

Key Points

This drill emphasizes defensive positioning relative to passing support. The first defender closes space on the ball. The second and third defender cover the closest, most dangerous passing options. If done properly, the three defenders will surround the ball and cut off all passing options. The defenders will have to use the grid boundaries to aid in closing down options for the offense. Watch how the defense adjusts after each pass.

In the variation in which play proceeds to goal, the positioning of the second defender becomes more crucial. If the player with the ball beats the first defender on the dribble is the second defender in position to thwart further penetration?

Variations

1. Allow offensive players unlimited touches.
2. Have the offense play toward goal. Start with the ball at midfield.

Defending the Pass (3 vs. 5)

20 yards

15 yards

67 Marking Up

Purpose

To practice sorting out defensive responsibilities, making recovery runs

Organization

Use 5 attackers, 5 defenders, a goalkeeper; 5 attackers and 2 defenders start at midfield; 3 defenders start at the top of the penalty area. Position a server with a supply of balls behind midfield players.

Procedure

1. The server plays the ball into the space ahead of the five attackers. The attackers try to advance quickly for a shot on goal.
2. The defenders try to delay the attack, mark attackers, win the ball, and clear it back to the midfield.

Key Points

The defenders need to sort out responsibilities quickly. They collectively need to determine who is marking whom. The task is complicated by the fact that two of the defenders are making recovery runs. These players should pressure the ball if possible or at least try to get goalside of an attacker. The sweeper or other defensive players should help orchestrate the effort by yelling out instructions such as the following: "Watch the runner on the outside," "Step to the ball."

The defense has succeeded if the offense delays and the two defenders have time to recover.

Variations

1. Have the two defenders at midfield enter play on the first pass from the attacking team.
2. Have more of the defenders start on the midfield line (more defenders making recovery runs).

Marking Up

68 Forward First (5 vs. 5 Plus 4)

Purpose

To work on penetrating the ball to goal, passing to feet, moving off the ball, shooting

Organization

Use 14 players (2 teams of 5 on a small field 20 by 30 yards with full-size goals, 2 additional players from each team positioned on each end line); 2 goalkeepers.

Procedure

1. Each team tries to score on one of the goals.
2. The two extra players move along the end line and cannot enter the grid. They are not marked by defenders and cannot score but are used for penetrating passes. They must put the ball back into play with one or two touches.

Key Points

Players should look to use their teammates on the end lines at all times. Passing forward is the preferred option if possession can be maintained or a scoring chance is possible. The end-line players will need to work hard to get open. They should move back and forth on the end line to get into open passing lanes. Once the player makes the pass, teammates in the field will need to sprint into the space in front of the goal. Defensive pressure is high at this point, so players must go hard for the ball.

When shooting off a back pass, solid contact with the ball with the inside of the foot or the instep is more important than a powerful, driving kick. Encourage players to pass the ball into the back of the net.

Variations

1. Require a pass to one of the end-line players before a shot can be taken.
2. Give more points for a goal that involves a pass to the end line first.
3. Play with one end-line player per team. Set up two goals on each corner of the end line (four goals total per field). The end-line player plays between these two goals.

Forward First (5 vs. 5 Plus 4)

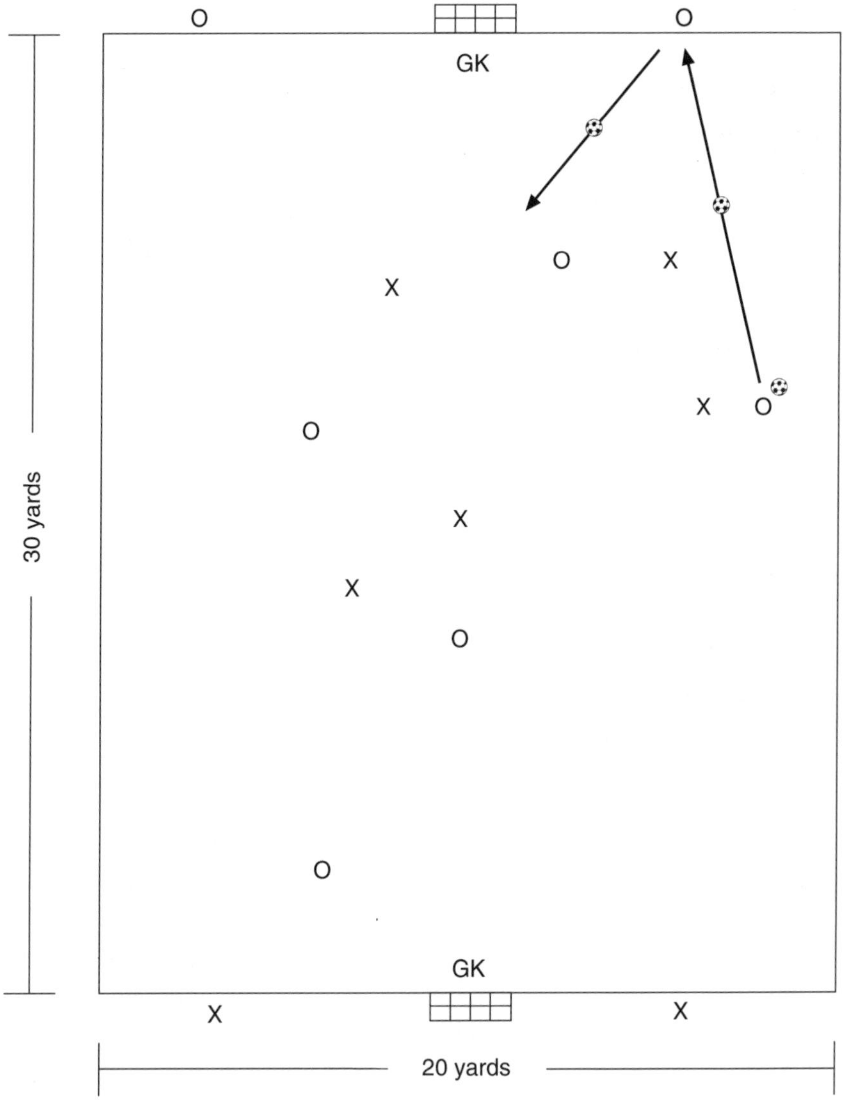

69 Thinking Player's Restriction

Purpose

To practice accomplishing specific tasks, thinking with the ball

Organization

Use 8 to 12 players (2 teams set up for regular scrimmage) on a full field or short field, depending on the number of players.

Procedure

1. Give each player a different restriction.
2. If a player violates the restriction, award the other team a free kick.
3. Suggested restrictions for individual players include the following:
    - One touch.
    - Two touch.
    - Three touch.
    - Can dribble only.
    - Can only pass forward.
    - Can only pass backward.
    - Must touch sideline after every pass.
    - Can only pass to a certain named player.
    - Can only receive a pass after three consecutive passes.
    - Cannot shoot.
    - Cannot call for the ball.
    - Add your own. Be creative!
4. See chapter 5 for further description of restrictions and conditions.

Key Points

Allow players a little time to adapt to the restrictions. The hope is that players will think twice before playing this first available option. They have to think about what their teammates can and cannot do given the restrictions and the relative situation.

Variation

Tell each player his or her restriction secretly. Don't allow players to tell teammates what their restrictions are.

Thinking Player's Restriction

GK

O O O

O O O

X X X

X X X

GK

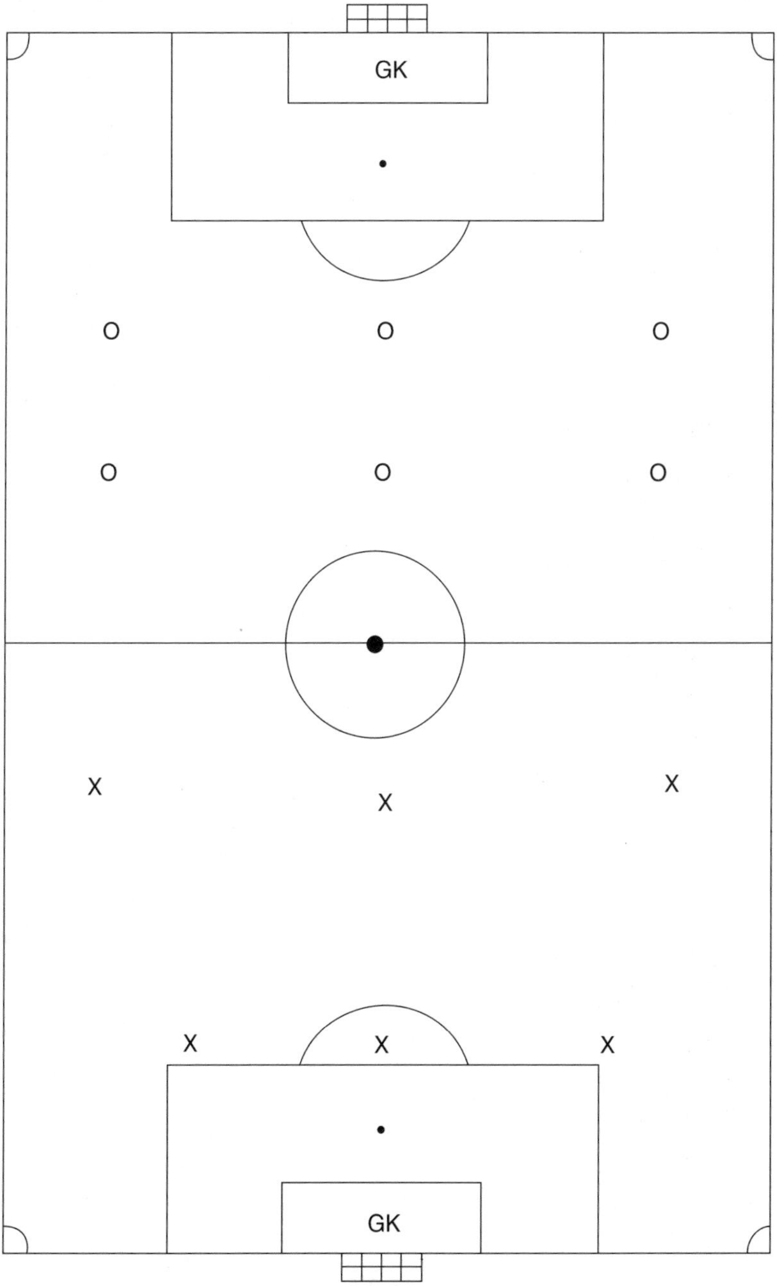

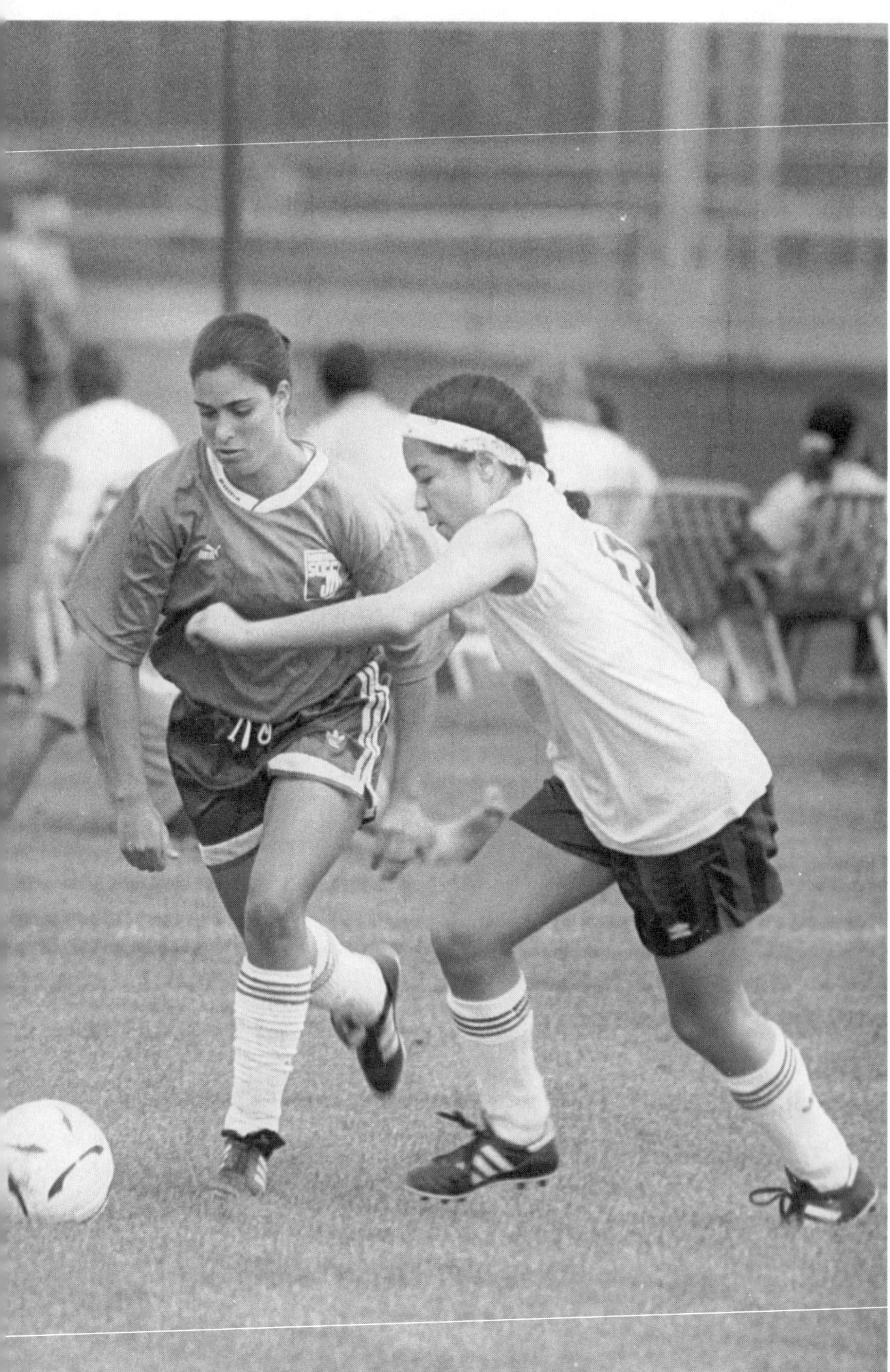

CHAPTER 5

Using Advanced Drills in Practice

The drills in this book explain to coaches how they can teach advanced soccer skills to their players. Each drill gives the purpose, the procedure, key points, and suggested variations. More important than any of this information is how you present the drills to the players during a practice. This chapter explains different techniques the coach can employ to help players develop these new skills. A section on restrictions helps to clarify why and when a coach can use *conditioned play* to enhance the learning process. The last part of the chapter provides a model for mixing and matching drills to form complete practices.

Whenever introducing a new drill or new skill to players, start by providing a context. Explain how the skill might be used in a game situation. Try to get players excited. Create an environment in which they are motivated to learn. Because players learn new skills in different ways, demonstrate and explain first-time drills. Give players time to experiment with the new material. Add instructions and increase pressure as the players get the hang of it.

Coaching Techniques

Coaches can use different methods to help players develop new skills. Following is a summary of some techniques. Consider using one or more of them as you introduce the drills in this book to your players.

Increase Difficulty in Steps

Break a concept or skill into stages or steps. Start with the most simple part, then progressively increase the pressure (by adding movement, restricting space, or increasing defensive pressure). To improve passing to forwards, for example, progress through the following activities during a practice: passing in pairs, passing in pairs while moving, passing combinations (drill 19), keep-away with target player (drill 55), point player (drill 57), and forward first (drill 68). See the following for more sample progressive practice plans.

Teach Skills Through Repetition

Have players perform fundamental skills and movements over and over. This is particularly useful when introducing a new skill. Many drills in this book highlight skills that are used infrequently in games. Let players practice these new skills in small groups to maximize touches on the ball. Even advanced teams can use repetition skill work to master fundamentals and improve players' comfort with the ball.

Freeze Play

As players are performing a drill, you can yell, "freeze" or "stop," then explain a concept or make a point. If a player makes a bad pass, for example, coach yells, "freeze." Everyone stops. Coach and players quickly analyze the situation and correct the mistake. Use this method sparingly so you don't disrupt the flow of the game unnecessarily.

Involve Players in Analysis

At the end of a pre-established time bring the players together and let them analyze what happened. After players perform a drill for 10 minutes, for instance, the coach brings the team together and asks, "How did it go?" "What did we do well?" "What do we need to work on?" This method helps players think on their own. Use it after games and scrimmages as well. Try to keep the conversation focused on specifics. Have players avoid criticizing each other or themselves.

Give Simple Instructions

As a rule, communicate only one or two ideas at a time to your players. Go for small gains each drill and each practice, and don't overcoach. Keep the sermons simple. Let players experiment with new drills for a while, then give explanations only as needed. When in doubt, encourage, instruct, or praise!

Assign Homework

Give players specific assignments to accomplish by the next practice. Introduce new skills in practice, then ask that players practice them on their own time. Choose a player at the next practice to perform the assigned skill for the rest of the group. Keep the players accountable.

Create a Competitive Environment

Structure the drills so that there is a winner and a loser. Award points for goals or successful attempts. Let players know where they rank relative to the other players on the team. You can find out, for example, who is the best 1 vs. 1 dribbler on the team by keeping score in facing a defender (drill 6). Each player keeps track of successful attempts. At the end, the coach records the scores and ranks the players. (You can also keep track of the best defensive tackler using this method.)

Use Video and Statistical Analysis

Objective feedback is a useful resource for players and coaches. Statistics are particularly useful to track player development over time. Keep statistics during games for each player. Count the number of good passes, shots on goal, defensive tackles won, and so forth. Be creative. Use a volunteer to help record the data. You can also record statistics for specific drills. Count success rates, and help players analyze what happened and why.

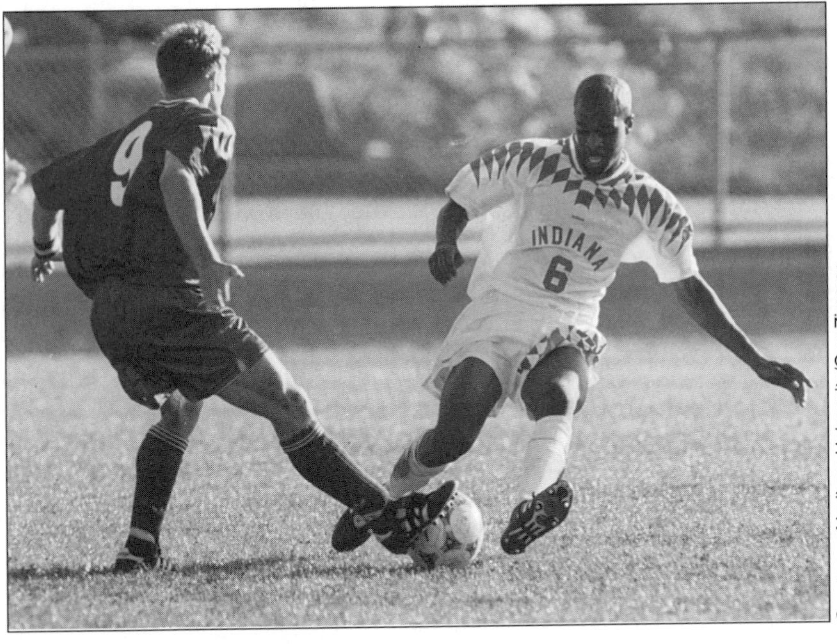

Courtesy of Indiana University/Guy Zimmer

Scrimmage Variations and Drill Restrictions

A particularly useful method for training the advanced player in specific techniques and even tactics is to require that they use them during a scrimmage. This type of practice activity is called the *conditioned* or *restricted* scrimmage. You can also apply restrictions in drills; for example, many drills in this book have built-in restrictions. Sometimes the restrictions appear under the variations. The restrictions and the purpose for each are summarized as follows.

One Touch

Players have to pass the ball away in one touch. Do not allow them to trap or control the ball then pass it. This restriction is extremely difficult to perform. All passes have to be nearly perfect. Players have to know where to pass before they receive the ball. This restriction forces quick movement off the ball as players must anticipate open passing lanes. Emphasize thinking ahead, field vision, and communication.

Two Touch

Players have to play the ball away in one or two touches. Allow a player one touch to control the ball and one touch to pass it away (or shoot). This restriction forces players to anticipate. They need to evaluate options quickly, preferably before the ball arrives at their feet. Supporting players also need to think ahead. They need to be available for passes before the two touches are spent. With this restriction, the first touch is crucial. Players must control and direct the ball so they can properly play the second touch.

Three Touch

Allow players three touches or less to play the ball. The restriction can also require the player to play the ball in exactly three touches (no more, no less). The second restriction emphasizes ball control and using nearby space.

Ball Below the Knees

The ball cannot be passed or played above the knees; preferably it is passed on the ground. This forces players to use supporting passing lanes and minimizes long kicks without a purpose. Emphasize giving support to teammates. Does the player with the ball have support?

Neutral Players

Add one or two players who play only offense. These players are on whichever team has the ball. Encourage teams to keep possession and not to force play. There is (in theory) always a teammate who is unmarked.

Keep-Away Games

In keep-away games players don't try to score on a goal. The emphasis is on possession. Players try to keep the ball away from the other team by moving into positions of support. Encourage players to keep width and depth in the playing area. Vary the size of the area and the number of players to emphasize different points.

No Tackling

Allow players to intercept passes but not to tackle the player with the ball. A two-touch or three-touch restriction should be in place to minimize dribbling. This restriction emphasizes defensive positioning. The first defender closes space on the dribbler and narrows the available options. The supporting defenders close off passing lanes. Use this restriction in drills to put less pressure on the player dribbling the ball.

Vary the Field Size

Always consider the size of the playing area. Is the field narrow, wide, long, or short? Typically, a larger space works to the advantage of the offense; less space favors the defense. When scrimmaging, a wide, short field will encourage crosses into the middle. A long, narrow field will require short passing combinations. In general, the smaller the space, the more control players must exhibit with the ball.

Practice Planning

Give careful consideration to each practice. Give players the opportunity to warm up, practice skills, and play in small-sided games. Relate everything to the game, and give a careful balance to drills and scrimmages.

The *progressive model* of practice planning is commonly used by competitive coaches. Players start practice with drills that have little or no pressure and maximum ball touches. They have an opportunity to warm up and practice skills. Later, you can add pressure. The pressure might be restricted space in which to perform a skill or drill or the added presence of a defender. Each step of the practice asks the players to take on new variables.

Practice might start with players working on individual skills. Later, players work in small groups. They perform skills against opponents. They make decisions. These practices build up to a scrimmage (with or without restrictions). In this phase, players work on skills under gamelike conditions.

The sample practice (pp. 152 and 153) below are examples of how to use the drills to form complete practices. They follow the progressive model and also match drills to specific objectives. Use the drill finder (pp. vi and vii) for other ideas about matching drills to specific objectives.

SAMPLE PRACTICE PLAN 1

Keeping and Winning Possession in the Midfield

Activity	Time required (min)
Warm-up, muscle stretches	15
Individual skills	
Shielding (drill 11)	10
Passing combinations (drill 19)	20
Break	5
Support passing with teammates	
Possession or punishment (drill 24)	15
3 vs. 1 squared (drill 28)	15
Midfielder with space (drill 64)	15
Break	5
Scrimmage	
Last goal wins (drill 54)	20
Total time	**2 hours**

SAMPLE PRACTICE PLAN 2

Defending the Attack

Activity	Time required (min)
Warm-up, muscle stretches	15
Individual defensive skills	
Fifty-fifty ball (drill 4)	10
Defender's dilemma (drill 10)	10
Team defense	
Defensive heading (drill 49)	15
Boxed in (drill 60)	15
Counterattack (drill 63)	15
Break	10
Scrimmage and small-sided games	
Forward first (drill 68)	20
Unrestricted scrimmage	10
Total time	**2 hours**

Courtesy of University of Portland Sports Information

CHAPTER 6

A 1 vs. 1 Player Evaluation Model

One drill in this book, drill 14, provides the basis for an innovative method of evaluating a group of 16 or more players. The model, as it is described here, ranks players as they compete in a series of 1 vs. 1 games. The results provide a quick and objective analysis of relative 1 vs. 1 soccer skills. You can use the process for player tryouts or for evaluating the players on an existing team. The coaches and the players (as well as other interested parties) will be able to clearly see how their performance ranks relative to the other participants.

Bob Livingstone of the Rockville Center Soccer Club in eastern New York State developed this method of player evaluation. Livingstone uses it for his club as well as for evaluating players for the region's Olympic Developmental Teams.

Using the basic setup as given in the 1 vs. 1 challenge, drill 14, create one playing field or station for each pair of players. If you have 40 players, for example, you'll need to set up 20 stations. Each station will have a pair of small goals made with cones or markers. Set the goals 5 yards apart (parallel rather than facing each other). Set each station 15 to 20 yards from the one before in a systematic fashion.

Livingstone and his colleague Dick Schroeder have found that 11 sets of competition are adequate to evaluate players. Any longer and injuries and fatigue take their toll. The players keep track of the score of each game. There are no referees. At the end of one minute, the loser goes back one station (to a lower numbered station); the winner advances (to a higher numbered station). Give a three-minute rest between rounds; then repeat the process. If the score of an individual game is tied after one minute, play continues with sudden death until a goal is scored. (Because fatigue is a concern, don't let one pair continue for too long. You might have to flip a coin to determine who advances.)

To win consistently players must have a combination of strength, speed, stamina, and agility. They must have strong dribbling and ball-control skills. They must demonstrate an ability to tackle and win the ball in 1 vs. 1 situations. This method also measures a degree of competitiveness (psychological), which is important for high-level play.

Use the results of this ranking along with other criteria, especially as the tryout progresses. The 1 vs. 1 challenge is not the final say as to the merits of an individual player. It is a way to identify players who have the base qualities needed for high-level play as measured against the relative abilities of their peers.

Keeping Score

To start, divide players randomly into starting positions. Record the starting position of each player. It doesn't matter where a particular player starts. Measure each player from his or her respective starting positions. Measure a player who starts on one of the bottom stations the same way as a player who starts at a middle or top station.

Although you can calculate the results by simply charting the players' positions at the first set and again after the last set, it is important to note the position of each player before each round. Doing this will eliminate errors and record the results of individual matches.

Treat the first and last stations different from the rest. At the top, the winner repeats the station; at the bottom the loser repeats the station. This will be important to note when calculating scores at the end.

If there is an odd number of players, rotate the winners out at the top station. One player sits out the first match and rotates in on the second. The winner of the previous game at the top station sits out the next game (see the example later in this chapter). At the end of all the games, go back and note how many rounds a particular player sat out. Some players will drop out due to injury or fatigue.

Sample Evaluation

The sample scorecard in table 6.1 represents the field notes from a tryout of 43 girls for an Olympic Developmental Team. Each player gets a number. Station 1 represents the bottom station; 21 indicates the top station. Because there was an odd number of players, the winner at the top rotated out after each match.

The columns indicate the individual matchups for each round of games. At station 1, round 1, player 4 played player 6. Player 4 lost the first game

Table 6.1 — 1 vs. 1 Player Evaluation Scorecard

Round/Game

Station	1	2	3	4	5	6	7	8	9	10	11	final pos.
1	4-6	4-14	14-20	14-12	12-20	14-20	20-30	46-20	52-46	52-56	52-66	66-72
2	12-14	6-20	4-12	18-20	14-22	12-30	14-46	30-52	56-20	66-46	56-72	52-46
3	18-20	12-22	6-18	4-22	30-18	46-22	12-52	56-14	30-66	72-20	12-46	56-20
4	22-24	18-30	22-40	6-30	46-4	52-18	56-22	12-66	14-72	12-30	14-20	12-98
5	30-32	40-24	30-32	40-46	52-6	56-4	18-66	72-22	18-12	14-40	30-98	14-92
6	36-40	32-44	24-46	32-52	40-56	6-66	4-72	6-18	40-22	18-98	40-92	30-110
7	42-44	36-46	44-52	56-24	32-66	40-72	6-32	40-4	6-98	22-92	110-18	86-40
8	46-47	42-52	56-36	44-66	24-72	50-32	92-40	32-98	92-4	6-110	22-86	18-
9	50-52	56-47	42-66	36-72	44-50	24-92	50-98	36-92	110-32	4-86	6-	22-116
10	54-56	66-50	72-47	50-42	36-92	98-44	24-36	110-50	36-86	32-	116-4	6-124
11	64-66	54-72	50-86	92-47	98-42	36-47	110-44	24-86	50-	116-36	32-124	4-112
12	72-74	86-64	54-92	98-86 → w	86-47	42-110	86-47	44-	24-116	50-124	112-36	32-78
13	86-88	74-92	98-64	96-54 → l	54-110	116-86	42-	116-47	124-44	24-112	50-78	36-47
14	92-96	88-98	96-74	110-64 → w	64-116	54-	116-64	124-42	47-112	44-78	24-47	50-108
15	98-102	96-104	88-110	116-74		64-118	124-54	64-112	78-42	47-118	44-108	24-118
16	104-106	102-110	116-104	108-88	118-74	124-108	118-112	78-54	64-118	42-108	118-64	44-126
17	108-110	116-106	108-102	118-104	124-88	104-112	108-78	118-104	54-108	106-64	126-42	64-106
18	112-116	78-108	118-106	124-102		74-78	104-120	108-126	106-104	126-54	106-128 ↑	42-54
19	78-84	118-112	124-78	112-106	102-78	120-88	126-74	106-120	84-126	120-104	84-54	104-128
20	118-120	124-84	128-112	126-78	120-106	102-126	106-88	84-74	88-120	102-84	88-104	74-84
21	124-126	128-120	126-84	120-128	126-84	128-106	84-102	128-88	102-74	88-128	74-102	88-102
22	128	126	120	84	128	84	128	102	128	74	(128)	
Notes:				96 injured	108 out 104 out 112 out					120 injured		

and stayed at station 1 for round 2. Player 6 won the game and advanced to station 2 for round 2. In round 2, player 6 played player 20. Player 20 lost her match at station 3 in round 1.

To determine a player's record, track the progression through each match. In the example, player 40 started at station 6, lost her first two matches, then won four in a row moving up to station 8. From there she lost three, won two, and ended up at station 7. Her record was six wins and five losses.

It is possible to calculate a player's score simply by recording the starting and finishing position of each player and by tracking the games in the first and the last station. If we look at 40 again, she started at station 6 and ended at station 7. She advanced one station in 11 matches. This indicates one win and leaves 10 games neutralized. For the 10 games, she had to move up as many stations as she moved down. In her case, she won five and lost five.

It is highly recommended that you record players' positions at the beginning of every round, as demonstrated in table 6.1. Doing so will allow you to recreate the entire competition. This is particularly important to avoid confusion and to track players who sit out games or drop out because of injury.

As players are injured or drop out, players and coaches will have to adjust accordingly. In this example, there was confusion between game 4 and 5. Livingstone let the players have an extended break after game 4, and several players did not make it back to the starting position in time for their games in round 5. Player 96 was injured in round 4. Round 5, therefore, was played without players 96, 104, 108, and 112 (as noted in table 6.1). Three of these players came back for game 6.

Livingstone did the best he could to fill up the stations and make adjustments on the spot. To do so, however, he had to mix up the regular rotation between rounds. Players 86, 54, 64 stayed in the same station for game 5 as they were in game 4. A notation on the grid shows whether they won or lost in round 4. Players 86 and 64 receive a *w* for a win. Player 54 receives an *exponent* (-1) because the game against 96 didn't count (96 was injured). This example shows why it is a good idea to record the starting position of each player at the beginning of each round. At the end, Livingstone could go back and recreate the win-loss record for each player (even though adjustments were made to the way players progressed from round to round).

Another way to handle players dropping out is to leave their space blank. Players keep the same rotation as if nothing happened. Some players will get a break, but this should not be counted as a win. Player 54, for example, in round 6 did not have an opponent. She ends up with two games not played (-2) because she rested this game, and she did not complete the game in round 4 when player 96 was injured. In round 7, player 54 moves up a station; the *empty spot* goes down a station. The rotation stays the same.

The last notation on the table occurs when 120 was injured in round 10. Livingstone could have left the spot blank for the last few games but instead chose to rotate player 128 at the top of the station into the empty spot.

Tabulating the Rankings

After the matches are completed, tabulate all results according to the number of games won, as in table 6.2. Assuming each player had the opportunity to play 11 games, list the number of wins for each player. Account for any matches that were not played because of injury or because the player rotated out by adding an exponent (-1). Player 84, for example, rotated out at the top station twice (-2). Therefore she played nine games, ending up with six wins and three losses.

When evaluating a player's record, pay close attention to the number of games not played. Looking further at the example, player 24 won all her games. Player 4 won 10 of 11 games while player 42 won 10 of 10 games. Of

Table 6.2 — Player Evaluation Results

Number of games won	Player #
11	24
10	4, 42 (-1)
9	6 (-1), 36, 44 (-1), 64, 74 (-1), 88, 102 (-1)
8	18, 32 (-1), 47, 54 (-2), 22
7	50 (-1), 104 (-1)
6	12, 14, 30, 40, 106, 84 (-2), 128 (-4)
5	
4	20, 120 (-3)
3	86, 108 (-1), 118, 126 (-1)
2	46, 56, 112 (-1), 78
1	52, 92, 96 (-8), 116
0	66, 72, 98, 110, 124

the players with nine wins, four of them (6, 44, 74, and 102) played 10 matches and had only one loss.

These top seven players were selected for the team after this tryout. The other three players with nine wins were earmarked for a confirming look at the next tryout. Those with six or more wins were asked back for another tryout. Those players with four or fewer wins were not invited back except for player 120, who missed three games due to injury.

Less than two hours later, 7 players had been selected and 18 were invited back for another look. The 18 had proven they were the most skilled in a high-pressure situation. They showed they had the base qualities for high-level play. The next phase of the tryout would be more traditional. The remaining players would be evaluated using a broader scope of activities.

About the Author

For more than 10 years Colin Schmidt has conducted soccer camps for players of all ages and abilities. The author of "Coaching Cards"—an innovative resource that features practice drills on pocket-size cards—he also has led coaching clinics for both new and experienced coaches. He is currently the director of coaching for an organization of 700 youth soccer players.

A former All-State and Olympic development player, Schmidt has played soccer for nearly 25 years. At Claremont McKenna College in California, where he played varsity soccer for four years, he was granted the "Alamshaw Award," an honor bestowed upon the one athlete who represents the best in community service. He is a member of the National Soccer Coaches Association of America and the Table Mountain Soccer Association.

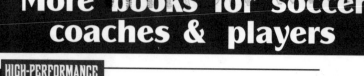

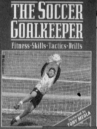